BROKEN TO BUILD
VOLUME TWO
THE WHOLE LIFE EDITION

"WHEN ME AND WOMEN BREAK"

A SPIRITUAL AND EMOTIONAL HEALING GUIDE FOR MEN AND WOMEN

Contents

Introduction

Healing & Wholeness/ When Men and Women Break

This book goes beyond just words on a page. It's an invitation—an honest, sometimes uncomfortable, but essential journey toward healing and wholeness. This continues the message begun in the 2024 book *Broken to Build*. Holistic Ministries facilitated the Broken to Build Healing and Wholeness Journey on Zoom, guiding participants through the book, devotional, journal, and Bible study curriculum. Initially open to women, now, as we move into Volume Two, it welcomes both men and women to walk through this together. Whether you're a man or a woman, the truth remains: life wounds everyone in diverse ways. Wounds often date back to childhood—silent cracks caused by neglect, trauma, rejection, or betrayal. Others stem from broken relationships, disappointments, or unhealed generational cycles that have quietly repeated over time. Sometimes, we don't even realize how fractured we've become until life demands strength from places we've ignored. But God knows. He sees every crack in your soul and every bruise on your heart. And He's not just interested in patching you up—He wants to make you whole. This book is for anyone brave enough to pause, feel, and heal. Throughout these pages, you'll find biblical truth, real-life testimonies from adults, and reflective prompts that invite deeper self-examination and spiritual growth. This isn't surviving. It's about transforming.

Men often carry their pain silently. They've been conditioned to believe that vulnerability equals weakness, and that showing emotion is a sign of failure. So, they bury their wounds beneath responsibility, busyness, or emotional detachment. Some mask their brokenness with work, achievement, or anger—believing that as long as they stay productive, the pain will remain hidden. Others build emotional walls so high and thick that even their closest friends can't see what's truly happening inside.

This is for the man who is struggling with identity wounds—questioning their worth, value, and place in the world. Some wrestle with unspoken childhood scars, never having words to describe the trauma they endured. Others are shaped by a culture that celebrates stoicism but punishes vulnerability. Behind the confident smile and strong exterior, many men are silently bleeding—dealing with emotional fatigue, depression, self-doubt, or unresolved anger that sometimes spills out uncontrollably. You are reading a book written for the man who's tired of pretending. Tired of carrying weight alone. Tired of smiling outward while breaking inside. It's for the leader who pours into others but feels empty in secret. It's for the son still grappling with wounds from his father, or the husband whose unhealed wounds are beginning to affect his marriage and family. It's for every man who senses God calling him to wholeness but isn't sure how to find that way.

Women often break in diverse ways—but just as profoundly. Many wears invisible capes of strength, holding families, ministries, and friendships together while secretly unraveling inside. Some numb up their pain with busyness, perfectionism, or by overextending themselves—saying yes to everyone else while saying no to their own emotional needs. For some women, brokenness appears as people-pleasing, overachievement, or remaining in toxic relationships just to feel wanted. Others carry silent grief from miscarriages, heartbreaks, betrayals, or words that wounded their identity years ago but still echo today. Some women struggle with feelings of never being enough—

never doing enough, never giving enough, never measuring up—regardless of how much they sacrifice or carry out. This book is for the woman who has been strong for so long that she's forgotten what it feels like to be nurtured herself. It's for the mother who holds her household together while neglecting her own self-care. It's for the friend who smiles in public but weeps in private. It's for the daughter still waiting for the affirmation she never received. It's for the wife who loves deeply but struggles to trust because of past wounds. Whether her pain comes from betrayal, abandonment, childhood trauma, or self-inflicted wounds—this book meets her where she's been bleeding silently. People break—but they often break differently. The symptoms may not look the same, but the root issue is universal: there are places in both men and women that God longs to heal. This journey doesn't shy away from that truth. It leans into it. The healing process may feel different for each, but God's invitation is for everyone: Come. Let Me heal the places you have hidden. Let Me touch the memories you've buried. Let Me restore what life, people, and circumstances have broken. Whether you're the man holding it all together for everyone else... or the woman smiling while silently bleeding... Whether your wounds are fresh or decades old... Whether you've named your pain or avoided it altogether... God is calling both sons and daughters back to wholeness. This isn't just a women's healing book. This isn't just a men's emotional guide. It's for the human soul—male or female—that's tired of pretending and ready for freedom. Healing isn't gendered. It's God's heart for every broken place. So, wherever you find yourself as you turn these pages—whether you're standing strong on the outside or already crumbling on the inside—know this: God specializes in healing both the seen and the unseen. Your story isn't over. Your healing is possible.

Let's begin—together.

Chapter 1: Identity After the Shattering

"When Brokenness Rewrites Your Name"

Before I formed you in the womb, I knew you, before you were born, I set you apart..."

— JEREMIAH 1:5

"I praise You because I am fearfully and wonderfully made..."

— PSALM 139:14

There is quiet violence that occurs when identity is shattered. You may still carry your name. You may still wear your smile. You may still function. But somewhere in the pain—after betrayal, failure, abuse, or sin—your sense of who you are begins to dissolve. We often associate identity with performance: the roles we fill, the accolades we earn, the relationships we manage. But when all of those break down, when what defined you falls apart—who are you then? Many of us often build our lives on a shattered identity. Is there anyone in this life who can honestly say that nothing and no one has ever shattered them? Please introduce me to that person, and I will say that such a person cannot be real. Shattered can be something that happened to you in the past, but it doesn't have to be what you use as a foundation for your life. Anyone going through life thinking that the life they planned will one day disappoint them—think of that as the script you wrote for your own life, which you're reading with regret and shame. But if you're reading this, I want to introduce you to yourself and let you know that shattered is not your identity. Shattered is a breaking point—a fork in the road of opportunity for something new. Shattered is associated with destruction, with being unrecognizable. You try to pick up the pieces of this shattered situation, of the broken version of yourself, of the broken relationship, and you don't know where the pieces fit. How do I fit into this life I'm living now, which looks unrecognizable? I no longer recognize myself because the life that surrounded me is gone. The shattering is not the end; it's a sign of renewal. We must understand that God doesn't do anything or create anything without purpose. His ways are not ours, and His thoughts aren't ours. We need to recognize the urgency of the season we are in and move through it. Often, brokenness is identified with the name you've carried your entire life. It might not be your actual name, but it's a label you've given yourself over the years. Brokenness can shatter your dreams and make your future seem bleak, with no hope for survival. Do you even know yourself anymore? The answer is no, and that must change. Rewriting your story is not negotiable when God is the author. This reminds me of Moses receiving the Ten Commandments—to establish a foundation of principles under God's law. The law was written to ensure that when the Israelites entered the promised land, they would have a firm foundation. But to Moses' surprise, when he returned from the mountain, he found that instead of patiently waiting and praying, they had begun to build a calf, worshipping a god who was not the true and living God who had delivered them. They used material things—gold, jewelry—to do it. In our lives, we sometimes decide not to value certain things because we want quick relief from pain. So, we sacrifice instead of giving our brokenness to God. Material possessions can be replaced; they have no real value because they are not alive. We are the ones who bring life to everything lifeless. If you have an outfit or shoes, they hang in the store until you decide to buy them. Once you place value on them—whether it's your earned money or someone else's—they become valuable because of who is wearing them. The brokenness you feel is not inherently bad; it becomes useful when you overcome what tried to shatter your identity. Often, if something was shattered, it was false—any actual value God gives to you cannot be broken. There is no false deity or power that can destroy what God has placed in and on you. Sometimes, the false narrative and false name we believe don't hold value when we carry them. When Moses received the Ten Commandments a second time, God wrote them Himself because the first set had been broken—they were unreadable. Moses believed the people, given their actions and spiritual state, couldn't comprehend what God was giving them, so God rewrote the tablets. Your name is what defines you; it's not connected to what has been shattered, but to where you are going.

Some identities don't just disappear. They shatter. And when they do, we begin to pick up false labels:

"Unlovable."
"Damaged."
"Used."
"Unworthy."
"Too much."
"Not enough."

This is the quiet war of the soul. And it's one the enemy hopes you'll fight without realizing it's a battle at all. There has been an identity theft: not just a crime, but a crisis. The enemy of your soul has one consistent mission: to confuse you about who you truly are. If he can make you believe you're beyond repair, then he can delay your purpose. This tactic dates to the Garden. In Genesis, Eve is tempted by the serpent not just to do something wrong, but to doubt something true: that she was already created in God's image.

- *The lie? "You're not enough as you are."*
- *The bait? "Become more."*
- *The result? Shame and hiding.*

Shame has always been the enemy's favorite tool. Because shame doesn't say, "I did something bad."

It says, "I am bad."

But here's the truth:

- You are not your brokenness.
- You are not what happened to you.
- You are not what you did in your darkest moment.
- You are not what others failed to see in you.

The beauty of God's rewriting is that it is never about erasing the past. It is about redeeming the past and giving it new meaning. When God rewrites your name, He does not just give you a fresh start; He gives you a new story. One that no longer carries the weight of the shattered pieces you once had. This latest story is not dependent on your strength, your performance, or your past successes or failures. It is written in the ink of grace, mercy, and divine purpose. Think about the prodigal son in the Gospel. When he returned home, broken, and ashamed, his identity as a lost son was still valid, but that was not the whole story. His father rewrote his name—not by ignoring the brokenness, but by welcoming him back with open arms and celebration, restoring his place as a beloved son. Your Heavenly Father does the same for you. Your shattered identity, your brokenness, does not define you—He does. One of the most incredible traps of shattered identity is the labels we accept—words like *failure, unlovable, weak, rejected, worthless.* These are not names God gave you; they are names the enemy whispers to keep your bound. But what if those labels are like the broken tablets Moses shattered? They are pieces of brokenness, fragments of lies that cannot hold the weight of truth. Just like God replaced the tablets with a new set, He offers to replace those false labels with truth.

Truth says: You are chosen.
Truth says: You are fearfully and wonderfully made.
Truth says: You are more than a conqueror.

These truths do not depend on your past but on who God is—and who He says you are. Rewriting your name is not instantaneous. It is a process, a journey that requires patience, faith, and often surrender. Just like the Israelites had to wait and learn before receiving the second tablets, you too must wait on God's timing and teaching. It may require you to:

- ***Let go of old identities that no longer serve you.***
- ***Allow God to heal the wounds that made those identities feel permanent.***
- ***Embrace a new narrative built on hope, purpose, and divine destiny.***

The journey may feel long and uncertain, but God's purpose is still steady. Your broken pieces are not thrown away; they are being gathered, refined, and repurposed. In the Bible, names carry power. When God renamed Abram to Abraham, it signified a new destiny—a father of many nations. When Jacob wrestled with God and was renamed Israel, it marked a new identity as a prince in God's service. When Jesus named Peter, he declared him the rock upon which the church would be built. What would it mean for you to receive a new name from God? Not one based on your past mistakes or others' opinions, but a name rooted in His purpose and love. It could be Redeemed, Beloved, Heir, Child of Promise, or New Creation. Naming is an act of authority. It's God's way of saying: "This is who you really are." And with that name comes the power to walk confidently into the future, no longer haunted by your shattered past. You may wonder, "But how do I live beyond what shattered me?" The answer is in surrender and faith. Surrender your brokenness to God, not as a burden but as an offering. Faith isn't pretending pain doesn't exist but trusting that God can and will transform it. The apostle Paul, who went through many hardships, wrote, "Therefore, if anyone is in Christ, the new creation has come: The old has gone, the new is here!" (2 Corinthians 5:17). Your shattered identity is the "old." It doesn't have to define your future. God's rewriting is a call to hope, renewal, and wholeness. It's a call to embrace the divine purpose that is still intact no matter how broken the journey has been.

Consider Sarah's story. She grew up feeling unworthy because of childhood rejection and years of verbal abuse. For decades, Sarah carried the label of "broken"—a name she accepted as truth. It affected her relationships, her career, and her self-image. One day, after a season of deep prayer and counseling, Sarah started to see her story differently. Instead of defining herself by rejection, she began to hear God call her "Beloved." Gradually, Sarah embraced this new name, and it became her identity. The broken pieces of her past no longer controlled her. She began to heal, to build, and to live with a new sense of purpose. God's truth rewrote her shattered identity, and with it came freedom.

How Do You Rewrite Your Name?

Reflect: What names or labels have you carried that do not align with God's truth? Write them down.

Repent: Ask God to forgive you for believing lies about yourself and surrender those labels to Him.

Receive: Claim the new names God offers in Scripture and in your heart. Speak to them aloud daily.

Renew: Surround yourself with people and environments that reinforce your new identity in Christ.

Resist: When old lies creep back, combat them with God's Word and the testimony of His faithfulness.

SCRIPTURES TO DECLARE OVER YOUR LIFE

"You are my beloved child; with you, I am well pleased."— LUKE 3:22

"I am the Lord who heals you."— EXODUS 15:26

"For I know the plans I have for you… to give you a future and a hope."
— JEREMIAH 29:11

"My grace is sufficient for you." — 2 CORINTHIANS 12:9

"I am God's masterpiece, created anew in Christ Jesus."
— EPHESIANS 2:10 / 2 CORINTHIANS 5:17

The beauty of God's rewriting is that it's never about erasing the past. It's about redeeming the past and giving it new meaning. When God rewrites your name, He doesn't just give you a fresh start; He gives you a new story—one that no longer bears the weight of the shattered pieces you once carried. This latest story isn't dependent on your strength, performance, or past successes and failures. It's written in the ink of grace, mercy, and divine purpose. Think about the prodigal son in the Gospel. When he returned home, broken, and ashamed, his identity as a lost son was still valid, but that wasn't the whole story. His father rewrote his name—not by ignoring the brokenness, but by welcoming him back with open arms, celebrating him, and restoring his place as a beloved son. Your Heavenly Father does the same for you. Your shattered identity and brokenness don't define you—He does.

One of the biggest traps of a shattered identity is the labels we accept—words like failure, unlovable, weak, rejected, worthless. These are not names God gave you; they are names the enemy whispers to keep you bound. But what if those labels are like the broken tablets Moses shattered? They are pieces of brokenness, fragments of lies that cannot hold the weight of truth. Just as God replaced the tablets with a new set, He offers to replace those false labels with truth.

Truth says: You are chosen.
Truth says: You are fearfully and wonderfully made.
Truth says: You are more than a conqueror.

These truths do not depend on your past but on who God is—and who He says you are. When we accept false labels, we live under a self-imposed prison. We act as if these names were carved in stone, immutable and unchangeable. But God's power to rewrite is greater than the enemy's power to lie. The key is to recognize those labels as lies, to refuse to identify with them any longer, and to embrace the truth God proclaims. Rewriting your name is not instantaneous. It is a process, a journey that requires patience, faith, and often surrender. Just like the Israelites had to wait and learn before receiving the second tablets, you too must wait on God's timing and teaching. It may require you to:

- **Let go of old identities that no longer serve you.**
- **Allow God to heal the wounds that made those identities feel permanent.**
- **Embrace a new narrative built on hope, purpose, and divine destiny.**

The journey may feel long and uncertain, but God's purpose is steadfast. Your shattered pieces are not discarded—they are being gathered, refined, and repurposed.

BIBLICAL EXAMPLES OF REWRITTEN IDENTITY

Abram to Abraham:

In Genesis 17, God changes Abram's name to Abraham, meaning "father of many nations." This name change wasn't just cosmetic. It signified a new identity rooted in God's promise of legacy and blessing. Abraham no longer carried the identity of a man without descendants but was given a new name that had hope, purpose, and divine favor.

Sarai to Sarah:

Abram's wife, Sarai, also received a new name—Sarah, which means "princess." This signaled a new status and a future in which she would become the mother of nations. God's renaming gave her a renewed identity beyond barrenness and disappointment.

Jacob to Israel:

Jacob, a man known for his struggles, deceit, and brokenness, wrestled with God and came away with a new name—Israel, meaning "he struggles with God." This name signified not only his personal transformation but also the birth of a nation and a covenantal identity.

Simon to Peter:

Simon, the angler, was renamed Peter by Jesus, meaning "rock." From a humble man of little influence, Peter was given a name that symbolized strength and foundational leadership in the early Church. His past failures did not prevent God from giving him a new identity and purpose.

These examples remind us that God's act of rewriting is a divine invitation to leave behind the old and step into the new. Your shattered identity is not the final word. God has a new name, a new story, and a new purpose for you. The Israelites' experience with the broken tablets is a powerful reminder of the importance of timing. Moses smashed the first tablets in grief and anger, but the second set, written by God Himself, symbolized patience, restoration, and readiness. Similarly, God's rewriting of your name happens in His perfect timing. You may be tempted to rush the process—trying to fix things on your own, patching together your broken pieces prematurely, or ignoring the pain. But rushing often leads to temporary fixes that don't last.

Instead, trust God's timing. Wait for His Word to inscribe your new name, your new purpose, and your new identity. Let this season of waiting be a time of deep healing, reflection, and growth. Faith is essential in embracing your rewritten identity. It is the bridge between your shattered past and your restored future. Faith says yes to what God promises even when your eyes cannot yet see it.

Hebrews 11:1 defines faith as "the assurance of things hoped for, the conviction of things not seen." You may not yet see how the broken pieces of your life fit together, but faith assures you that God is working behind the scenes. Faith also calls you to walk forward in obedience—taking steps to live out your new name even when the old identity tries to pull you back. It is faith that enables you to claim your place as a child of God, beloved and redeemed.

MATERIALISM AND FALSE IDOLS: THE FALSE GODS WE BUILD

The story of the golden calf in Exodus is not just a historical event but a spiritual warning for all generations. When the Israelites grew impatient waiting for Moses, they built an idol from gold, something tangible, visible, and powerful. In many ways, we do the same when our identity shatters. We replace God's truth with idols—money, success, relationships, approval, or possessions—that promise to fill the void but leave us empty. Material things have no actual power. They have value only because we assign value to them. But that value is fleeting and unstable. Actual value comes from God and the identity He gives. God calls us to surrender these false idols and to root our identity not in what can be bought or lost but in who God says we are. This surrender opens the door for God's rewriting to take place. After shattering, the unknown future can feel terrifying. The familiar is gone. The path ahead is unclear. But God's rewriting invites you to step into this uncertainty with courage. Remember Joshua, who took over Moses' leadership. God repeatedly commanded him, "Be strong and courageous." Why? Stepping into your rewritten identity often requires leaving your comfort zone and familiar broken patterns. The new identity is like a seed planted in fertile soil. It may be hidden for a while, but with time and care, it grows into something beautiful and strong.

PRAYER

If you are holding onto the broken pieces of your past, take a moment now. Imagine God reaching out His hand to you, offering to sign your name anew. What new name do you hear Him whispering over you?

Lord, I surrender my brokenness to You. I ask You to rewrite my name, not based on what I have done or what has happened to me, but on who You created me to be. Help me to see myself through Your eyes—loved, chosen, and whole. Give me the courage to walk into the new story You have for me. Amen.

TESTIMONY: LOST IN LOVE, FOUND BY GRACE

Her Story: She was the "strong friend." The dependable one. She held everyone together—until she lost herself in a string of toxic relationships. Each man she gave her heart to demanded more and offered less. She bent herself to fit their brokenness, believing that her value came from how much she could endure. At the end of one particularly devastating breakup, she stood in the mirror and didn't recognize herself. Her light was gone. Her voice is quiet. Her boundaries, erased. But it was in that silence, in that fragile moment, that God spoke a word she hadn't heard in years:

"Daughter."
Not "used."
Not "too emotional."
Not "foolish."
But Daughter.

It wasn't instant. But the healing started there. God didn't restore her identity by handing her a new relationship. He gave her a new mirror: His Word. And through that mirror, she saw her value—scarred, yes, but sacred. Loved not because she had never been broken, but because she was His. Your identity isn't something you build from scratch. It's something God *reveals* as you return to Him.

Psalm 139 says you were "knit together" in your mother's womb—knitted with detail, intentionality, design.

That means the truth of who you are was woven in *before* the trauma, before the rejection, before self-hate, before the shame. Your job is not to *create* identity; it's to *recover* it.

TESTIMONY: LOST IN CONFUSION, FOUND IN PURPOSE

His Story: He was raised in love. Rooted in church. Surrounded by people who poured into him—yet he always felt different. Born with a mental illness, he questioned why his mind didn't work like his siblings'. He watched them move with ease while he struggled in silence, wondering what was wrong with him.

Comparison became his mirror. He measured himself by what he couldn't do and assumed purpose belonged to others. He didn't know then that his siblings carried struggles too—just hidden in different ways. His battle was simply more visible.

But in the quiet moments, as he drew closer to God and began reading His Word, something shifted. God revealed a truth he had never been told:

"Son."
Not "broken."
Not "defective."
Not "less than."

But Son.
The change wasn't instant. But the healing began there. God didn't restore his identity by removing the struggle. He gave him a new lens:

His Word. And through it, he saw himself clearly—different, yes, but designed. Chosen not because he was without weakness, but because he was His.

Psalm 139 declares we are "fearfully and wonderfully made"—made with intention, before the struggle, before the comparison, before the questions. Your identity was woven in before the diagnosis ever had a name. Your job is not to create purpose. It's to recover it.

Ask Yourself:

1. What labels have you worn that God never gave you?

____

____

____

____

____

____

____

2. Who (or what) have you allowed to define your worth?

____

____

____

____

____

____

____

3. When was the last time you asked God to remind you of your name?

____

____

____

____

____

____

____

Journaling:

"God, show me who I am to You. Strip away the lies I've believed and reveal the truth I've forgotten..."

____

____

____

____

____

____

____

____

____

____

____

____

____

____

____

____

____

____

Rebuilding Begins with Believing

The truth is: healing identity doesn't begin with therapy, accountability, or affirmations. Those things are powerful and needed—but they're not the starting place. Healing identity begins when you believe what God says is true, even when everything in you screams otherwise.

"Let God be true, and every man a liar."

— ROMANS 3:4

When life has whispered lies long enough, you start repeating them to yourself like vows:

"I'll never let anyone hurt me again."
"I don't need anybody."
"I'll prove I'm worth it."

But the Gospel doesn't call you to self-protection or self-promotion—it calls you to **surrender.** God doesn't just want to *fix* your identity. He wants to **restore** the real one—the one that was buried under pain, performance, and pressure.

THE PROCESS OF RECLAIMING IDENTITY

Let's talk. What does reclaiming your identity in Christ look like?

1. Confront the False Narrative

Ask yourself: What lie have I believed about who I am?
Use Scripture to challenge that lie directly.

LIE	TRUTH
I'm unworthy.	You are chosen and royal (1 Peter 2:9).
I'm broken beyond repair.	He restores your soul (Psalm 23:3).
I'm a mistake.	You were fearfully and wonderfully made (Psalm 139:14).
I'm not enough.	His grace is sufficient (2 Corinthians 12:9).

2. Grieve the Loss

This part is often overlooked—but it's vital.

It's okay to grieve the version of you that was built around survival, not wholeness.

Let God meet you in your grief. Your tears are sacred to Him (Psalm 56:8).

3. Speak the Word Over Yourself

Identity must be declared. Every day, speak these truths:

- I am a child of God (John 1:12).
- I am no longer a slave to fear (Romans 8:15).
- I am seated with Christ in heavenly places (Ephesians 2:6).
- I am forgiven and free (Romans 8:1).

God's workmanship (Ephesians 2:10).

Speak to them until they sink in. Then speak to them some more.

4. Redemption Is Personal

God doesn't mass-produce healing. His custom fits it. He knows your story. He knows the exact moment your identity started to fracture. And He knows how to bring you back to life—not just functioning, but whole. When Jesus met Peter after the resurrection, Peter was still carrying the weight of failure. But Jesus didn't call him by his shame. He called him by his future:

"Feed my sheep."

He restored his identity by restoring his purpose.

God does the same for you.

A PRAYER FOR REDISCOVERING YOUR IDENTITY:

Abba Father,

Confess that I have let life, people, and pain define me.

Worn labels You never gave me.

Spoken words over myself that You never spoke.

Hidden behind false strength and pride, afraid to be seen.

Today, I choose to believe that You are the Author of my identity.

Reclaim that which was stolen.

Restore what's been ruined.

Speak over me again the name You gave before I was ever broken.

Surrender the version of me that was shaped by wounds.
And I receive the version of me that was formed by Your hands.
In Jesus' name, Amen.

Write a letter to your younger self—the version of you who first started questioning their worth.

Then write a letter to your future self, declaring who you are becoming in Christ.

YOUNGER____

____
____
____
____
____
____
____
____
____
____
____
____
____
____
____
____
____
____
____
____

FUTURE

FINAL DECLARATION: Brokenness distorts identity, but God restores it through truth. Your identity is not defined by your worst moments, but by God's eternal design. Healing requires grieving the false self and reclaiming the true one through Scripture, prayer, and belief.

Chapter 2: The Man/Woman in the Mirror

"Seeing Yourself Through God's Eyes"

"Anyone who listens to the word but does not do what it says is like someone who looks at his face in a mirror and, after looking at himself, goes away and immediately forgets what he looks like."

— JAMES 1:23–24

"Therefore, if anyone is in Christ, he is a new creation. The old has passed away; behold, the new has come."

— 2 CORINTHIANS 5:17

When you look in the mirror, not just the physical mirror, but through your spiritual lens—what do you see? Usually, we see ourselves as others see us, as if through their lenses. We are often labeled by our giftings—what we can do. Labels like doctor, lawyer, physician, nutritionist, counselor, and, in the church, pastor, bishop, apostle, and prophet define us. Then there are labels based on abilities—singing, making clothes, planning, and administration. While it's good that others see these giftings and recognize them as real because you have the ability, the real question is: how do you see yourself? Even when you look in your physical mirror every day, are you pleased with what your life reflects? Many of us dislike how we look physically. We study and alter our appearance, and we see people around the world undergoing surgeries to change their looks. Sadly, some even lose their lives or suffer physical distress trying to see a different reflection. Others steal identities, using social security numbers, names, credit, and more. Some steal ideas because they believe copying others will grant them the same recognition and attention. The only mirror you should use to judge how you look and how your life appears is God's eyes. Busy people who fly across the country for ministry or business trips often become fixated on seeking validation and on wanting their gifts to help others or companies.

We can recognize ourselves in the mirror because others are pleased with what we offer. But what happens if all of that is taken away? What if people don't call? What if they don't need you? What if they disapprove of what you're giving? Will you still feel the same about the person you see and the inner person you grapple with daily? There comes a point in everyone's healing journey when the actual confrontation begins—not with your past or others, but with yourself. Looking in the mirror becomes more than checking your appearance. It becomes spiritual. It's standing face to face with what you've carried, who you've become, and who God still calls you to be. Told you this: looking in a physical or spiritual mirror and understanding what you see—past or present—can help you, whether the reflection is good or bad, to take the next step. You can't adjust your course if you don't know where you are now. Building a church or ministry without assessing what goals to set in the next three months, or what they're for, won't get you far. Are you aiming for bigger things, or are you just seeking results to meet others' expectations? Are you truly doing that for which you were created? Accepting who you really are is the only way to find satisfaction when you look in the mirror next. Whether that means adjusting, changing your appearance, or even looking unthinkingly, where you must regain your sight to truly see, hear, and encounter God, when you understand that everything you are and will become is made in God's image. Seeing is believing, but faith involves evaluation. You don't assess your standing by what you see; you evaluate it by what God says. You don't honestly see without a revelation of what you're looking for. When Jeremiah was asked by God what he saw, he was challenged to see differently. He was not to focus on being too young or unqualified. God already knew what He placed inside Jeremiah; He just needed him to see and understand it. He required him to evaluate properly with a new lens. God says He is changing your spiritual lenses so you can see as He sees. You had to reach a breaking point for this to happen. So, if you're looking at shame, guilt, or despair—if that's your current view—that's okay. That is your assessment right now. But God says, Look again. This time, you will see the original designer's plan; you will see His intended purpose. Some paths you took were led by God, others not. Still, when you finally align with His will for your life, everything will work together for your good, as Scripture says: "All things work together for the good of those who love the Lord and are called according to His purpose." Not only do we have purpose, but when we love Him, He said, "If you love me, keep my commandments." Loving God makes it harder to disobey Him. We need His love to love Him as He desires. God so loved the world that He gave His only Son. That's why He gives us Himself in the person of the Holy Spirit. When we don't know how to love, and our capacity to love runs out, He takes over and loves through us. When you see yourself, you see God. When people meet you, they experience God. They should leave your life changed. The transformation begins now.

What do you see when you look in the mirror?

Some see shame. Others see strength—but not the peaceful kind. The kind forged in fear and fueled by survival. Some look at themselves and feel lost—like they're still becoming, still recovering, still unknown. And for some, the mirror shows nothing. Just numbness. Disconnection. Fog. But the Word of God tells us we are to look deeply and not forget what we've seen—not just physically, but spiritually.

- ***You were made in the image of God.***
- ***You were broken, yes, but not abandoned.***
- ***And God doesn't just want to heal your view of Him—He wants to heal your view of you.***

Some people stare into the mirror and only see failure. They rehearse mistakes from years ago like they happened yesterday. Others stare and only see what others have spoken over them—negative words that stuck like glue to their identity. "You'll never be good enough." "You'll always struggle." "You're too much." "You're not enough." These labels become internal dialogue, looping in the background of your mind like a broken record. But let me tell you something: God's mirror doesn't speak like that. His mirror speaks truth and grace. His mirror reflects not just who you've been, but who you're becoming. It reflects potential, redemption, and destiny. But before you embrace that image, you first must confront the false ones you've believed for too long. Some of us have gotten used to living with distorted reflections. It's like wearing cracked glasses and assuming everyone else's vision is just as blurry. We measure our worth by likes, follows, compliments, and opportunities. We tie our value to external applause. But here's the reality: Applause fades. Platforms shift. People change their opinions. God's perspective stays the same. So, what happens when God begins to strip away the false mirrors? When he starts dismantling the image you've worked so hard to project? That's when the real work begins. That's when healing begins. He doesn't do it to shame you. He does it to reveal the real you— the version of you that was fearfully and wonderfully made before life started layering on masks. And here's the truth: Sometimes God will lovingly disrupt everything you've built around a false identity. He'll allow people to misunderstand you. He'll close doors you once depended on for affirmation. He'll cause certain assignments to dry up—not because He's punishing you, but because He's rescuing you from a life of performance-based worth. God wants to pull you out of cycles where you feel valuable only when you're producing or being praised. You are more than what you do. You are more than your last achievement. You are more than the labels—whether they're good or bad—that people have placed on you. God calls you His own. And sometimes the scariest thing is learning how to be loved without performing for it. Let that sink in: Can you rest in being God's child, even when you're not being noticed? Even when you're not being called on. Even when others are not affirming you. This is the mirror work God invites us into. It's where identity gets redefined. It's where healing becomes personal. It's where titles, accomplishments, and public image no longer define your private worth. The hardest part of healing is the silent season—the time when God hides you. The calls slow down. The texts stop coming. The invitations dry up. You wonder if you've been forgotten. But what feels like isolation is divine separation. God is pulling you aside not to punish you, but to prepare you. He's silencing the noise so you can finally hear His voice about who you are. There's beauty in the hiding place. It's where identity is reborn. It's where you realize that your value was never in the mic, the boardroom, the pulpit, the classroom, or the applause. Your value was always in being His. And for some, God is asking you to lay down even good things. Things you've worked hard for. Things you've prayed for. Ministry roles. Business titles. Leadership positions. Not because they're bad—but because they've become your mirror. Somewhere along the way, you started seeing yourself more through your work than through His Word. You've become more attached to your assignment than your identity. God loves you too much to let that continue. When you look in the mirror, and all you see is exhaustion, burnout, or emotional detachment, it's a signal. It's heaven's way of saying: "You've been running empty, trying to earn what I've already given you." You don't have to prove your worth to God. You don't have to perform for His love. You don't have to strive to be seen. You are already seen. You are already loved. You are already chosen. The mirror God holds up shows you as a son. As a daughter. As a vessel of purpose. Not perfect but perfectly loved. Not flawless but fully redeemed. And yes, there will be hard moments in this process. The days when you want to run back to the safety of your old labels. The moments when your flesh wants validation from people more than affirmation from God. But stay with the process. Stay in the reflection room. Stay with the Holy Spirit as He heals your sight. Because the next time you look in the mirror... You won't just see scars. You'll see survival. You'll see strength. You'll see someone who didn't quit. Someone God still has plans for. This is what happens when you start seeing yourself through God's eyes. This is what happens when distorted reflections become divine revelation. So, as you turn the page... Pause for a moment. Breathe. And ask yourself: "What mirror have I been looking in?" "And am I finally ready to see myself the way God does?"

But before you can fully embrace this new vision, there's one more layer that often needs to be peeled back: the fear of starting over. For many, the hardest part isn't believing that God loves them. It's believing that they can begin again. That after years of mislabeling, masking, and misidentifying, God still has room for them in His story. Starting over sounds good when preached from a platform, but when it's your reality—when you're the one having to let go, rebuild, and relearn who you are—it can feel terrifying. You wonder, where do I even begin? How do you rebuild when everything you thought defined you has been stripped away? How do you navigate relationships when people only know the outdated version of you? How do you step forward when shame keeps pulling you back? This is the space where grace meets grit. This is where faith becomes more than a concept. It becomes oxygen. God never asked you to rebuild with your own strength. He asked you to say yes. To show up in the process. To trust that even when you feel lost, He is not lost concerning you. He knows where you are. He knows how to get you from here to healed. There's a beautiful truth tucked inside this hard season: God does His best work in empty spaces. The emptiness you feel. The loneliness? The confusion? It's a room being cleared for clarity. The shedding of old identities makes space for the new. When Gideon was threshing wheat in hiding, afraid and unsure, the angel of the Lord still called him "mighty warrior." Long before Gideon ever stepped onto a battlefield, God was calling him according to his destiny—not his current fear. And God is doing the same with you. You may feel like you're still in the shadows. Unseen. Unnoticed. But heaven is speaking over you. The Holy Spirit is whispering identity to your spirit. Not based on what you've done but based on who you are. God's original design is coming back into focus. The layers of shame are falling. The masks of performance are being removed. Even the internal vows you made in survival seasons—those promises like "I'll never trust again," "I'll never let anyone in again," or "I'll just stay in the background where it's safe"—God is challenging those, too. He's not asking you to pretend those moments didn't happen. He's inviting you to send them. To lay down every self-protective wall that's kept you from fully seeing yourself and fully receiving His love. This is your permission to break the agreements you made with fear. It's your invitation to stop defining yourself by your worst day or your biggest failure. It's your release from cycles of people-pleasing and performance-driven living. You don't have to hustle for worth anymore. You don't have to wear false strength like armor. God is calling you back to authenticity—the kind that doesn't need applause to feel affirmed. The kind that doesn't crumble when opportunities slow down. The kind that knows how to sit still in God's presence and know that being loved is enough. There is healing in the stillness. There is identity waiting for you in the silence. And when you look in the mirror next time, you may still see some scars. You may still remember the seasons that hurt you. But you'll also see something else... Hope. The quiet kind that rises in the morning before the sun comes up. The gentle kind that reminds you: Your story isn't over. Your reflection is being rewritten.

TESTIMONY: HIDING IN PLAIN SIGHT

Her Story: She felt as though she had to hide her gifts. Even though she lacked confidence in the abilities God placed inside her, those very gifts made others around her feel jealous and intimidated. Their envy and resentment often showed in subtle ways—whispered comments, distant behavior, silence instead of support. Though unsure of herself, she still moved forward with grace, trying to find who she was along the way.

She threw herself completely into accomplishing goals, believing that her gifts, talents, and the anointing God placed on her life were all that defined her. At times, she felt seen. She felt validated. She even felt celebrated—but often by others, not by herself. And then came the devastation. The deepest wounds were not from strangers, but from the very people closest to her. In front of her, they celebrated her. Behind her back, the conversations changed.

If only they could see my pain. If only they understood that I don't even love myself. If only they knew how depressed I was, how many nights I prayed for life to simply go away.

But then—something shifted.

As she began to draw closer to God, she learned something life-changing: she was loved and valued beyond her gifts, beyond her performance, and far beyond what others thought of her. The jealousy she once feared, she now understood—for beneath envy often lies admiration.

With this revelation, she decided to transform what had once broken her. Instead of shrinking, she began to shine. Instead of feeling threatened, she began to encourage. She looked at those around her—the same ones who once resented her—and whispered from her healed place:

"YOU CAN DO IT, TOO."

TESTIMONY: DAMAGED BEYOND FIXING

His Story: He had the titles. The house. The degree. The accolades. But none of it silenced the emptiness he carried. He had learned how to smile without joy. Lead without vision. Serve others without ever really showing up for himself. From the outside, he looked whole. Respected. Admired. He was the dependable one. The fixer. The one everyone called when they needed advice, money, or a solution to their crisis. He took pride in being strong—the man who could hold it all together no matter what life threw at him. But when he stood alone, just him and the mirror, he saw someone who had mastered performance.

Eventually, the facade cracked. Not publicly, but internally.

He started asking questions that success couldn't answer:

"Who am I really?"

"Why am I doing all this?"

"What would be left if I stopped performing?"

And it was in that unraveling that God gently met him. Not with shame. But with truth:

"You don't have to earn love here. I've already called you Mine."

But what no one saw was the cost of that strength. Behind the steady voice and problem-solving exterior was a man stretched thin... emotionally bankrupt and spiritually disconnected. He wasn't sleeping well. He avoided being alone with his thoughts. The weight of unspoken disappointments, silent grief, and years of emotional neglect began to press harder with every passing day. He kept telling himself, "Just push through... You don't have time to fall apart." But the truth was—he already was... just slowly, quietly, where no one could see. One evening, after another phone call from someone needing something from him, he sat in his car long after the engine stopped running. Staring at his reflection in the rearview mirror, with tears he didn't expect, he finally admitted what he'd been running from: "I'm tired... and I don't even know who I am outside of fixing things for everyone else." And in that still, vulnerable moment, God met him. Not with more demands... not with a to-do list... but with an invitation:

"Son... It's time to let me carry you. You don't have to hold it all together anymore."

The Process of Becoming Honest to Yourself:

1. No More Pretending:

True healing begins when you stop hiding from God, from others, and from yourself.

We often carry the weight of pretending:

- *Pretending we're not hurting.*
- *Pretending we're over it.*
- *Pretending we've moved on.*

But God doesn't heal what we hide. He heals what we hand over.

Ask yourself:

Am I living from a place of truth or image?

____

____

____

____

____

____

What parts of me do I hide, even from God in prayer?

____

____

____

____

____

____

Where have I forgotten who I am?

____

____

____

____

____

____

2. **You Are More Than the Mirror**

The physical mirror shows your appearance.
The mirror of the Word shows your identity.

James 1 describes the one who hears God's word but doesn't live it out as someone who sees their face and forgets. But those who look intently into the law of liberty—God's Word—walk in freedom and transformation. When you stare long enough into the truth of God, the lies lose their grip.

"You will know the truth, and the truth will set you free."

—JOHN 8:32

A Prayer for Restored Sight

Father,
I've hidden from myself for too long. I've let shame rewrite my self-worth. Today, I chose to look in the mirror—not just with my eyes, but with my heart.
Show me who I really am, beneath the pain, beyond the rules.
I surrender the mask, the pressure, the perfection.
Teach me how to live as a new creation—not in name only, but in truth.
Amen.

Ask Yourself:

1. What part of yourself have you been hiding from?

____

____

____

____

____

____

2. What do you see when you look at yourself, and how does that differ from what God sees?

____

____

____

____

____

____

3. Reread 2 Corinthians 5:17. What "old" parts of you are you ready to release?

____

____

____

____

____

____

Journaling:

"God, here is what I see when I look at myself... but help me see what You see."

____

____

____

____

____

____

____

____

____

____

FINAL DECLARATION: Restored sight brings clarity to you and makes it easier to identify where you are going. You will no longer try to see yourself through a broken mirror. The mirror broke a long time ago. God says, "Stop trying to pick up the old, broken you—the news you are being revealed."

Chapter 3: Healing Masculinity & Femininity

The Wound Beneath the Role

"So, God created mankind in His own image, in the image of God He created them; male and female He created them."

— GENESIS 1:27

"Husbands, love your wives, just as Christ loved the church and gave Himself up for her..."

— EPHESIANS 5:25

"She is clothed with strength and dignity; she can laugh at the days to come."

— PROVERBS 31:25

We have learned how to be people through survival, not through Scripture. We grew up mimicking what we saw, not always what was healthy. Some of us have never seen what a godly man or woman looks like. Others had examples but watched them fail, fracture, or disappear. What we inherited emotionally, relationally, and spiritually shapes our understanding of gender identity far more than we realize. Regardless of the good examples we have, all of us in creation are flawed. The only true reflection by which we can really live is God. And while

He knows all of this, He still gives godly examples that lead us to Him—the Perfected One. Some people don't even have the privilege of having a positive role model in front of them throughout their entire lives. They've never seen a model of healing. They've never seen what it looks like to walk in identity. And they're left wondering if they're the problem, when in reality, they simply never had the picture.

Do we get to decide? Absolutely not.

When we reach the age where we can make our own decisions, when we move out of our parents' house and start our own families, we begin to see the good in the not-so-pleasant ways we have acquired throughout our lives. It's not until we start leading that we see how much we inherited. There is not a man or a woman that I have met who could have actually predicted or even foresaw the brokenness they developed from childhood up into adulthood, and how difficult it is to unpack all of those areas and find out the root of why you do what you do, say what you say, and act the way you act. There are pieces buried so deep in the past that you don't even know they're shaping your future. The only person who can do that is supernatural. It is our Almighty God. This is why we have to allow the Word to wash us and make us whole, and the power of God to transform us. Because with all the advice, with all the counseling, with all the manufactured principles put in place, there is a supernatural occurrence that happens to help all those things. Healing is not just intellectual or spiritual. God makes the rules and defines the role. Man tries to conduct and administer. And while that can be noble, sometimes it's a mixture—our opinions, our wounds, and what we think is wisdom—blended with God's intended design. That's why confusion enters where clarity should reign. We are expected to carry out roles we are built for—so you have the little boy and the little girl, wounded and never afforded the opportunity to fully accept who they are, while a responsibility is placed on them to perform, not to live in. Do not walk in with confidence. Just perform. And when performance replaces identity, pressure replaces peace. That's why so many break down under roles they were never prepared for. Not because they're weak—but because they were never taught how to be whole. They were never given the space to say, *"This part of me is still healing."* But God sees the little boy and the little girl inside of you. And he's not asking you to fake strength anymore. He's asking you to be still long enough to be rebuilt. So, if you've been surviving instead of living, mimicking instead of becoming, performing instead of walking confidently in who God created you to be—know this: You don't have to carry that pressure anymore. You don't have to stay trapped in patterns you never chose but inherited.

God wants to introduce you to who you were before the survival kicked in. Before the example failed. Before the role became a burden.

- *He wants to show you the man.*
- *He wants to reveal the woman.*
- *He wants to restore the design.*
- *He wants to rebuild the child.*

Some men were told, "Be tough. Don't cry. Provide. That's enough."

Some women were told, "Be pretty. Be pleased. Don't speak too much."

And slowly, without realizing it, maturity became about pressure, and womanhood became about performance. But God's image is not fractured. It is complete. And He made both men and women to reflect His glory in diverse ways, but equally valuable, powerful, and needed. Healing your identity as a man or a woman means peeling away distortions, confronting pain, and returning to your original design.

You've been living in a body shaped by battles. Carrying responsibilities with cracked hands and a tender heart. The truth is, you've done the best you could with what you were given—but that doesn't mean you were given enough. And that's not your fault. This is why God steps in—not to shame the survivor, but to heal the soul underneath. You weren't created to live in survival mode forever. God never called you to build your life on instincts that were formed in trauma. He's calling you ***out*** of reaction and ***into*** revelation. Because now that you know better—now that you see the pattern—He's permitting you to break it.

You are not the failed example that raised you.
You are not the broken mold you came from.
You are the redeemed vessel God is restoring.

And while you can't go back and rewrite the childhood, you can take what you've learned and allow God to rewrite the future. No more building with broken definitions of maturity or womanhood. No more measuring your worth by how well you hide your hurt. No more shrinking beneath roles that never fit right in the first place. God is not asking you to perform. He's inviting you to come. This is the invitation of maturity: not just to grow older, but to grow truer. To heal the child, honor the calling, and step boldly into the identity you were born with, not the one life forced on you.

The world told you to survive.
God is calling you to live.

Healing in this area begins with heart excavation, not just behavior change. God is after the root, not merely the visible fruit. It's possible to seem functional while internally fractured—leading, parenting, serving, and smiling—yet still carrying an unseen limp. This unspoken reality affects both men and women. They show up. They fulfill their roles. They meet demands. But beneath the surface, there's a longing for more peace, freedom, and authenticity. That's where God begins His healing—right in the places we've learned to ignore. Some men have built identities around control because it felt safer than vulnerability. They were taught that softness equals weakness and that silence equals strength. So, they became providers without being present, protectors without emotional availability. They wore armor but never allowed themselves to take it off. For women, the story isn't much different— just expressed in a different language. Many became nurturers for everyone but themselves, champions of others' dreams while burying their own. They learned to smile through exhaustion, pour from empty wells, and apologize for wanting more. Somewhere between childhood and adulthood, femininity became linked with performance and silence. But God is breaking that cycle. He's reaching into the places you've silenced—the tears you quickly wiped away, the disappointments you never voiced, the anger you suppressed because it didn't seem "godly" to show it. He's saying to both His sons and daughters: "I see you. I see the part of you that's still questioning if it's safe to feel, trust, and try again." The beauty of God's healing is that it isn't rushed. He doesn't force you into wholeness but invites you into it—layer by layer, revelation by revelation, surrendered wall by surrendered wall. He knows how to speak to the little boy behind the grown man's eyes, how to reach the little girl beneath the strong woman's smile. And he's unthreatened by your process. What seems like a delay is often divine protection. Some people you sought affirmation from couldn't handle the weight of your healing journey. The spaces you tried to find identity in weren't built to hold your vulnerability. And that's okay. Their inability doesn't mean you're unworthy.

In His wisdom, God gently pulls us into seasons where He becomes the only voice loud enough to redefine us. It's in these quiet seasons that we unravel layers of identity—roles accepted to feel valuable, titles chased to feel seen, behaviors adopted to feel safe. But now, God calls us to something deeper. He says, "You don't have to keep proving your worth." Whether you're a man who's led from emotional shutdown or a woman serving from depletion, this is your invitation to heal—to sit with God and ask the questions you've avoided or been too afraid to ask: Why do I respond this way? Why do I keep repeating these patterns? Why does love feel distant? Why does rest seem like laziness? Why does vulnerability feel dangerous? These questions aren't signs of failure but signals that your heart is finally ready to confront what's been carried too long. And in that confrontation, God will meet you—not with condemnation but with compassion. His Spirit will reveal the moments that shaped you—the unmet needs, buried grief, disappointments brushed aside but never released. Healing masculinity and femininity isn't about swinging to extremes or becoming hyper-masculine or overly feminized. It's about alignment—divine alignment—where who you are reflects the heart of the Father; where strength doesn't have to roar to be real; where tenderness isn't weakness but proof that your heart is alive and reachable. For men, healing might look like learning to speak when you prefer silence, asking for help when everything in you says, "Manage it alone," feeling without shame, loving without walls. For women, healing might look like allowing yourself to be helped, setting boundaries without guilt, crying without labeling yourself "too emotional," and trusting that God loves who you are when you're doing nothing at all. There's a sacred unraveling happening in your heart right now. God is gently pulling apart the lies woven into your identity—lies that say strength equals emotionlessness, being loved means being perfect, and that your value depends on productivity. Those lies are breaking—one by one. God is replacing them with truth, grace, and a new vision of being His child—whole, restored, and becoming. Don't rush this process. Let the tears come if they need to. Allow the questions to surface. Let the Holy Spirit guide you back—not to dwell in pain, but to reclaim the parts of your heart you left behind. Healing masculinity and femininity doesn't mean becoming someone you're not. It means returning to who God designed you to be all along—before trauma, before expectations, before roles distorted your reflection. This is your mirror moment—an opportunity not just to see yourself but to embrace yourself fully: the healed man, the healed woman, the image-bearer, the son, the daughter—loved by God all along, even while you were still trying to figure it out.

Testimony: When Femininity Is Fractured by Performance

Her Story: She grew up with a single mother who had no room for softness. Life was about survival, so she became tough, independent, and emotionally guarded. She heard "Proverbs 31" and rolled her eyes—because it felt like a checklist, not a gift. Being a woman meant multitasking, suffering silently, and keeping everything together.

She could lead. She could earn. But she had forgotten how to receive, how to rest, how to simply be. Her breakthrough came in prayer when God said, "You don't have to work for love, you already are."

It shook her—not because she didn't know it, but because she had never believed it deep in her bones. Her journey wasn't about becoming more feminine in appearance, but in spirit—in softness, in joy, and in learning to be held by the Father again.

The Holy Spirit reveals that femininity includes wisdom, strength, discernment, and glory.

God created male and female in His image—not to compete, but to complement; not to dominate, but to reflect. Jesus showed us that masculinity includes servanthood, tears, tenderness, and sacrifice.

When adults embrace their identity through God's lens, not culture's, healing flows.

TESTIMONY: WHEN PAIN MASKS MASCULINITY

His Story: He believed being a man meant providing and protecting. That's what his father taught—through presence, but not affection. When emotions surfaced, he stuffed them. When conflict arose, he either shut down or exploded. Vulnerability felt like weakness, and weakness was unacceptable. But beneath the silence was a deep longing to be seen, not just needed. He wanted to lead with love, not just responsibility. He yearned to be a better father, love more deeply, and express himself more—yet he didn't know how. His healing began the moment he heard a pastor say, "You don't have to be hard to be strong." That statement cracked something open inside him. It allowed him to be masculine and tender, powerful and present. He started to pray differently. Not, "God, make me a better man," but,

"God, help me become a healed man."

Healing masculinity means...

Embracing vulnerability without shame.

Leading with love, not fear.

Knowing your worth beyond performance.

Healing femininity means...
Owning your voice without apology.
Receiving love without earning it.
Standing strong without becoming hard.

Ask Yourself:

For Women:

Where have I had to "earn" love?

____
____
____
____
____
____

Have I embraced the truth of my worth apart from what I do?

____
____
____
____
____
____

Do I know how to rest and receive as a daughter of God?

____
____
____
____
____
____

For Men:

What lies have I believed about what it means to be a man?

____

____

____

____

____

Where have I buried emotion out of fear?

____

____

____

____

____

____

What example of maturity shaped me—for better or worse?

____

____

____

____

____

A Prayer for Healing

Father,
You created me in Your image, not culture's.
Heal the broken ways I've viewed myself as a man/woman.
Break every lie I inherited from pain, absence, or dysfunction.
Restore the original blueprint you placed on me. Help me not to compare or compete, but to live fully as You've made me.

Release the pressure to prove and receive the peace of just being.

Let my identity reflect Your glory—not performance, not pain, no pressure.

Just presence. Just purpose. Just You.

In Jesus' name, Amen.

Journaling:

"God, what do You want to heal in my understanding of manhood/womanhood?"

"What would it look like for me to reflect Your image more fully, starting today?"

____

____

____

____

____

____

____

____

____

____

____

____

____

____

____

____

____

____

____

____

____

____

____

____

____

____

____

____

____

____

____

____

____

____

____

____

____

____

____

FINAL DECLARATION: Be determined that your name has changed from titles to purpose. While purpose is the partiality of your existence, the person you become is beyond visibility; it's the state of being and authority.

Chapter 4: The Power of Safe Spaces
You Weren't Meant to Heal Alone

"Carry each other's burdens, and in this way, you will fulfill the law of Christ."

— GALATIANS 6:2

"As iron sharpens iron, so one person sharpens another."

— PROVERBS 27:17

Wholeness is not a solo journey. Even though your pain may have come through abandonment, betrayal, judgment, or rejection, your healing will still come through people. Not perfect people, but **safe** ones. God never intended for healing to happen in isolation. He is a relational God, and He designed us for connection, not control, community, not concealment. But here's the problem: When people have hurt us, we build walls instead of boundaries. We keep everyone at a distance—even those God sent to walk with us. Healing doesn't just require time; it also depends on the environment. The right environment—what we'll call a "safe space"—can be the difference between surviving and transforming.

You're not just living this life for yourself—you're living for yourself and for others. That's why God declares, "I'm the God of more than enough!" He never intended for us to survive off spiritual crumbs or just enough to get by. We are to live in the overflow—overflow of time spent in His presence, overflow of revelation, overflow of grace, and understanding that doesn't just fill us, but spills into the lives of others. To seek Him means to acquire, to gain, to discover, and to desire. He is my heart's desire, which is why I continue to pursue Him. It's never enough for me—I long to release myself, to give Him all of me, to know Him, and through Him, to understand the full expression of who I am and who I can become in Him. Want to pour myself out before Him and ask, "Will you trust Me?" That is the voice of the Lord. But here's the tension—your flesh can't trust Him. Your spirit may be saved, but your soul is still healing. The soul, the seat of memory and emotion, harbors past wounds that create internal conflict. That's where disconnection happens—not because God isn't near, but because old wounds are still speaking louder than His presence.

God is calling His people back. He's saying, "Stop deserting Me for people and things that mean you no good. And even for those that do have a purpose in your life—put them in their proper place." No relationship should carry more weight than your time with Him. Sometimes, wounds are what tie you to people. Other times, it's their good qualities. But in either case, God is calling us to healthy connection—no more codependent cycles. No more shared dysfunction. "You hurt, I hurt, we hurt"—that's not the design of a godly relationship.

Think about the pool of Bethesda. They were all gathered, waiting, hurting, and stuck. But none of them could help each other. Healing came from outside of that circle. Someone who was not part of their condition—Jesus—stepped in and administered healing from a place of wholeness. And even after the miracle, Jesus followed up with this: "Go and sin no more, lest something worse come upon you." That wasn't a threat, it was a warning. Sometimes it's not the obvious signs that trip us up. It's the small foxes—the unseen things. The little compromises we think don't matter. What opens the door is rarely the storm—it's the small crack. It's the "innocent" conversation, the unchecked pattern, the unhealed trauma. It's not always something everyone can see outside. And while I can't say with certainty what the man at the pool had done before, Jesus' words remind us that there are things in the natural—and spiritual—that give legal access to more damage. So, if God is telling you to walk away, release it—do it. There's a purpose behind every instruction. If He's saying, "Leave it alone," it's because He sees the whole picture. You don't have to understand the full why. Just know this—whether it unfolds now or later, ignoring the voice of God will always produce something for which you weren't ready. So, trust Him. Obey. And feast in His overflow—not just for you, but for everyone connected to your healing.

Healing was never meant to stay contained. It's not just about personal restoration—it's about collective transformation. There are people connected to your healing that you haven't even met yet. Your obedience doesn't just unlock doors for you; it opens pathways for others to be freed. This is why the enemy fights your wholeness so hard—because your healing becomes a testimony, and your testimony becomes a lifeline for someone else. You are not simply walking out of pain—you are walking others out with you. That's why the overflow matters. That's why the process matters. When you choose to stay in broken patterns, you prolong not only your own delivery but also delay the ones assigned to your journey. God is strategic. He places healing in community because He knows that connection activates accountability, and accountability cultivates transformation. But we must be willing to be seen. We must be willing to be known—not by everyone, but by someone. Safe spaces are sacred. And in a world full of filters and performance, finding people you can bleed in front of without judgment is a divine gift. Don't despise it. Please don't run from it. Don't let past betrayal rob you of present healing. God will send the right people—not to fix you, but to walk with you while He does. Because wholeness was never designed to walk out alone. Isolation breeds imagination, and imagination without revelation leads to deception. You begin to assume, to misread, to pull back. But in this season, God is calling you to lean in. Trust again. Not just in people—but in the God who sends them. His overflow isn't blessing—it's about building. And this time, He is building something you won't have to rebuild later. Let Him finish it. Let Him fill it. And let your healing speak—not just for you, but for generations after you. Here is something sacred about being truly seen and still fully loved. It is the kind of healing that can't happen in silence. The kind that refuses to take root in isolation. God never wired us to do this by ourselves, and though our wounds often tell us otherwise, the truth stays: we heal in community. We thrive in spaces where honesty does not feel like a risk and where weakness isn't viewed as a liability. Some of us have spent years hiding behind smiles, behind titles, behind responsibilities, carrying silent battles because we believed no one could handle our truth. But God, in His mercy, is now bringing you to a place where hiding is no longer a choice. Not because He wants to expose you to embarrassment, but because He wants to expose you to healing. Safe spaces are not perfect; they're intentional. They are marked by grace, by truth, by consistency. The people God assigns to walk with you in this season will not always have all the right words, but they will have the right heart posture. They will not always fully understand your pain, but they'll sit with you in it. They'll offer presence when solutions feel premature. They'll speak life when all you can hear is defeat. But for that to happen, you must first let them in. That's the battle for many—learning to trust again. Learning to open your heart again. Learning to risk vulnerability after betrayal. But here's what you need to remember: Not everyone is them. The people who wounded you before aren't the same people God is sending now. Discernment is key, but so is openness. If you shut everyone out, you block the very connections God wants to use for your healing. Safe spaces aren't found by accident; they're found through prayerful discernment and spiritual alignment. God has a way of sending divine relationships at the most unexpected times. A coworker who suddenly becomes confident. A neighbor who unexpectedly speaks about life into your situation. A stranger at church who prays over you with tears in their eyes as if they've known your struggle for years. These are not coincidences. These are orchestrated moments, designed by a God who sees exactly where you are and knows exactly what you need. And sometimes, the safe space you've been praying for doesn't come to look like a conference or a retreat. Sometimes it's found in the quiet corner of a coffee shop, during a late-night phone call, or on a worn-out couch where a friend says, "You don't have to explain. I'm here." And still, there will be moments when God becomes your only safe space. Seasons where no human presence seems available. Where no one seems to understand. Where the phone stays silent, and the inbox stays empty. Don't despise those moments. In them, God is training your heart to anchor itself in Him. Teaching you that before you run to people, you must learn to rest in His presence. Before you unload your heart to others, you must first learn to cast your cares at His feet. This balance—between divine intimacy and human connections where lasting healing takes place. Too much isolation, and you risk emotional numbness. Too much dependence on people, and you risk idolizing human affirmation. But when God becomes your anchor, and people become His instruments, you step into a rhythm of healing that's both heaven-led and earth-supported. In safe spaces, correction doesn't come as condemnation; it comes as compassion. Accountability isn't about control; it's about love in action. Encouragement isn't laced with performance-driven expectations; it's drenched in understanding and grace. And yes, even in safe spaces, conflict can arise. Misunderstandings happen. Feelings will suffer. But here's the difference: In a God-ordained safe space, people fight for resolution, not for ego. They apologize quickly. They listen deeply. They ask tough questions not to interrogate but to intercede. They speak truth, even when it's uncomfortable, because they care more about your growth than about keeping temporary peace. This is a kingdom connection. This is what God has in mind when He calls us the body of Christ—various parts, divergent functions, but one heartbeat. Your healing journey may require you to unlearn isolation. To renounce inner vows that say, "I'll never trust anyone again." To dismantle mental agreements that tell you you're safer alone. Yes, self-preservation feels protective, but it's also suffocating. Growth happens when you allow your heart to breathe again in the presence of those God has sent to walk with you. Healing happens when you stop rehearsing old betrayals long enough to recognize new blessings. There is a circle for you. A remnant of people who will cover you in prayer, sit with you in silence, challenge you in love, and celebrate you in progress. You don't have to have everything to be loved there. You just must be willing to show up. To stay. To let yourself be known. Healing in safe spaces also means being that space for others. You may not have all the answers, but your availability can save someone's life. Your listening ear can interrupt their spiral. Your text message can remind them that they matter. God doesn't just want you to receive healing from community; He wants you to release healing through community. You've been called to be both a recipient and a resource. As God pours into you, pour into others—not from a place of obligation, but from overflow. You don't have to be perfect or to be impactful. You must be present. So, as you walk this chapter of your healing journey, ask God to highlight the people assigned to your next level of healing. Ask Him to give you discernment for safe spaces and courage to step into them. Ask Him to prepare your heart to both receive and release. Because healing is contagious. Freedom multiplies. And when one heart finds a breakthrough, the ripple effect can change families, churches, cities, and generations. The enemy's goal was to isolate you in silence. But God's goal is to place you in a circle that calls you back to life. This is the power of safe spaces: when two or three are gathered in His name, healing becomes inevitable. Love becomes undeniable. And transformation becomes unstoppable.

What Is Safe Space?

A safe space isn't just a location, it's a posture. It's a relational atmosphere where you can:

- **Be vulnerable without fear of being shamed.**

- **Speak honestly without being silenced.**
- **Ask questions without being judged.**
- **Be corrected in love, not condemned in pride.**

Safe spaces are created by people who know how to listen, not fix. Hold space, not control it. They don't rescue you—they walk with you.

Testimony: When Women Found Safety in Sisterhood

Her Story: She never liked women's groups. Too much drama. Too much pretending. She had been burned by gossip and hurt by comparisons. So, when her friend invited her to a healing group for women, she hesitated.

But she went—halfhearted, arms crossed, ready to leave early.

And then it happened:

One woman shared her story—raw, unfiltered, honest. Another woman cried while praying for someone else. No one tried to gain an advantage over. No one tried to teach. They just showed up.

Week after week, she returned. Walls dropped. Heart opened. Healing began.

That group didn't fix her—but it gave her a space where healing could finally breathe.

Testimony: When Men Let Their Guard Down

His Story: He grew up in a house where emotions were dangerous, and silence was survival.

As an adult, vulnerability made him feel weak—even though he was dying on the inside.

A mentor invited him into a small circle of men who met monthly—not to talk sports or strategy, but to discuss soul matters. At first, he felt exposed. But then he heard a man say, "I'm struggling." And no one flinched. That broke something in him. For the first time, he didn't have to perform. He didn't have to impress. He could just be—and be accepted.

FINDING & BUILDING YOUR SAFE SPACE

If you've never had one, it can feel unsafe to pursue a safe space. But it starts with a few simple steps:

1. Ask God for discernment.
   Not everyone is meant to hold your healing. Ask God who you can trust with your story.
2. Start small.
   One friend. One counselor. One group. You don't need a crowd, you need connection.
3. Be honest about your needs.
   Safe spaces thrive on truth. If you need prayer, say so. If you need silence, that's okay too.
4. Give what you want to receive.
   Be a safe space for someone else. Offer presence. Offer grace. Offer confidentiality.

Ask Yourself:

1. Who in your life has made you feel seen, heard, and safe?

____

____

____

____

____

____

2. What walls have you built out of fear that might need to come down?

____

____

____

____

____

____

3. What's one step you can take to build a safe space this month?

____

____

____

____

____

A Prayer for Safe Relationships

Father,

I thank You for being my ultimate safe place—my refuge and my hiding place.

I confess that I've built walls where You wanted bridges.

I've stayed isolated when you called me into the healing community.

Please help me to recognize safe people.

Help me become a safe person.

Heal my fear of vulnerability.

Replace my defense mechanisms with discernment.

Lead me into relationships where I can grow, rest, and be known.

And where can I offer the same to others?

In Jesus' name, Amen.

Journaling:

"God, show me the people in my life who are safe—and give me the courage to lean into them."

"What would it look like to let someone in again?"

____

____

____

____

____

____

____

____

____

____

____

FINAL DECLARATION: God releases the people in your life to help along the journey. Some stay for the long haul and some come in for portions of your life.

Chapter 5: Forgiveness That Frees

The Unseen Prison

"Then Peter came to Jesus and asked, 'Lord, how many times shall I forgive my sibling who sins against me? Up to seven times?'
Jesus answered, 'I tell you, not seven times, but seventy-seven times.'"

— MATTHEW 18:21–22

"Bear with each other and forgive one another... Forgive as the Lord forgave you."

— COLOSSIANS 3:13

Forgiveness doesn't always feel like freedom. Sometimes, it wants to surrender the one thing we still have: our pain. After betrayal, abandonment, or deep offense, forgiveness can want to let someone off the hook. But here's the truth: forgiveness is not about them. It's about you. Your peace. Your freedom. You're healing. Unforgiveness doesn't keep them bound—it keeps you imprisoned. We have many moments in time. Some are devastating. Some demolish prison doors. The tangible presence of God marks some. Some change our lives forever—in clever ways, and sometimes not so good. But this moment, this time in your life, is destined to shift something—no more seasons of up and down. No more gaining momentum only to lose it. We can never let our fire dim. The enemy is patient. He waits until we are ready to move forward and make progress, and then he strikes. But God wants us free so He can elevate us. He cannot elevate darkness. All alliances with the enemy must be severed. The enemy looks to strip us of our authority, but God has already blessed us in advance. So, we go back. We go back to the foundations. God knew some of us would be born into chaos. He knew your grandparents or great-grandparents made covenants, erected evil altars, betrayed people, and shed innocent blood. He knew generational curses and patterns would try to follow you. But he also knew you were called to break them. He knew it would be a fight for you to discover your value. He knew you'd have to war for your divine inheritance. The enemy knows too. That's why he keeps sending the same spirits in different disguises. But God says, "I'm giving you strength to break free from Egypt." The Egypt of your past. The Egypt of your childhood. The Egypt of your trauma. He's saying, "I'm freeing you." He knew you would need help, so He sent Jesus. Jesus bore every sin, every betrayal, every abuse, every word curse, every generational curse, every secret pain. He bore it all so you wouldn't have to. And when you accept Jesus as your Savior, you put on the armor. You gain access to spiritual authority. You have discernment. You learn to recognize the enemy's tactics. God raises prophets and prophetic voices to help us see, to warn us, to align us with His will.

So don't believe the lies. You are not defeated. You are still not stuck. You may be in it physically, but spiritually, you are already free. God has given you keys—keys to open the prison doors. When Jesus got up from the grave, the veil was torn. We gained access. Death, hell, and the grave became powerless. The sting of death is gone. The enemy's weapons are powerless. The enemies' influence is ineffectual and made to confuse and discourage—but they won't work. Jesus has overcome the world. We will face suffering, yes. But we will persevere. We will overcome. You are not just building a life—you're building a legacy. A lasting testimony. That's why the enemy wants to trap you in cycles. But we are breaking them. I had to go back. I had to get to the root. When I was five years old, I witnessed my mother attempt suicide. Fear gripped me. I felt rejected. I felt abandoned. That moment marked me. It created a pattern. Years later, I attended a delivery service, and the Holy Spirit took me back to that very moment. I curled into a fetal position as the minister prayed. That little girl inside me needed to be healed. After my parents separated, abandonment layered upon rejection. Relationship after relationship repeated the same pattern. Even after salvation, the residue remained. The weight of it all was heavy. But Jesus already paid the price. I just had to apply His blood to my wounds. The blood of Jesus is like a gift card we don't use. It's there. It's paid in full. But we must apply it. Take every trauma, every memory, every injustice to the courts of heaven. Apply the righteousness of God. The courtroom of heaven is where justice meets mercy. That's where freedom happens. We must release every generational burden—even the ones we didn't choose. Even the traumas we narrowly escaped still leave scars. But Jesus heals even those. Understanding that unusual parts of us need freedom, our hearts, our souls, our minds, our memories—is key. Present your whole self as a living sacrifice. Ask God to free your mind of repeated thoughts, your heart of unforgiveness, your soul of trauma. This is how we become free.

And as you read this, speak these truths aloud. Don't just think about them declaring them. Release them because freedom has already been bought. Now it's time to walk in it.

Your foundation is now free, but Forgiveness is not the finish line—it's the foundation. Once you forgive, the real work begins. And that work is rebuilding. It's stepping into the space that offense used to occupy and saying, "God, fill this with purpose." It's recognizing that forgiveness didn't erase the memory—it just released the weight. Now that the prison door has been opened, the question becomes: ***What will you build on the other side?***

You've spent years managing the pain, organizing the trauma, supporting emotional walls like bricks in a fortress. But now, God is inviting you to use those same hands—not to guard yourself, but to build again. This is holy ground. This is fresh territory.

You'll have to learn how to trust again. How to speak without suspicion. How to walk without the limp of bitterness. You'll have to train your heart to believe that joy is safe. That peace is not just a moment, but a mindset. And even if it feels foreign at first, God is patient—He walks with you, brick by brick, healing by healing. This is the beauty of God's process: He doesn't just tear down what was. He rebuilds something more substantial. What the enemy meant to fracture, God turns into a framework. What was once a trigger becoming a testimony. What once broke you becomes the blueprint for helping others rise. Forgiveness opens the gate, but obedience builds the house. And now it's time to start laying the spiritual foundation—one decision at a time. You are not just surviving – it's a declaration, not your comfort zone; it's your construction zone. After forgiveness, your soul leaves survival mode. But don't be surprised if you feel lost at first. When pain no longer leads the way, it can feel like wandering. But this isn't confusion, it's clearing. God is making room.

Survival builds fast and frantically. Healing builds slowly and firmly. So don't rush the process. You are not behind. You're not late. The pace of grace is perfect for the season you're in. This is where identity is rediscovered. Without resentment to distract you, you now get to ask fundamental questions: Who am I when I'm no longer angry? Who am I when I'm not protecting myself from a wound? What do I want in this season? This is also where relationships are re-evaluated. When you forgive someone, it doesn't always mean they regain access. Forgiveness is a gift; reconciliation is a process. And wisdom knows the difference.

So, build wisely:

- **Rebuild your habits.**
- **Rebuild your expectations.**
- **Rebuild your thought life.**
- **Rebuild your spiritual disciplines.**
- **Rebuild your language—what you say to yourself when no one is around.**

Don't just detox the wound. Redesign the structure. You are the house of God. What are you offering your life now?

Bitterness may have once decorated every room, but now you get to choose joy. Fear may have been the wallpaper, but now you get to paint the walls with freedom. Build a life that reflects the healing, not the hurt. You can become the answer you prayed for. Now that you've walked through the storm, it's time to become a shelter for someone else. This is the ministry of the healed. You're not just building a life after forgiveness; you're building a legacy. Everything God restores in you becomes a tool for restoration in others. Your life becomes a testimony that says, "Yes, healing is possible." And not just healing—but flourishing. Abundance. Purpose. Peace doesn't need conditions to survive. There's a depth in you now. A weight. A spiritual authority. Because you didn't just preach forgiveness—you lived it. And people may not understand your joy. They may ask how you can smile after all you've been through. They don't know the hell you walked out of. They don't remember the nights you lay awake praying to forget. But God does. And now He's trusting you with influence, testimony, and healing for others. This is why your healing had to happen. Not so that you could feel better—but so you could carry something for the next generation. So, your children could be free from what you had. So, your voice could carry weight in places where others still whisper in fear.

You're not just healed, you're commissioned.
You're not just restored, you're rooted.
You're not just forgiven, you're fruitful.

And when people ask you how you got here, you can say: "I forgave, and I rebuilt. And by God's grace, I'm still building."

The Unseen Prison	Walking in Freedom Daily by Forgiveness
Focuses on the weight of unforgiveness	Emphasizes spiritual
Emphasizes emotional bondage and generational cycles	Discipline and mindset alignment

Testimony-heavy and rooted in deliverance	Practical and devotional—day-by-day
Discussing the courtroom of heaven and trauma roots	Walk in grace
Focuses on the daily maintenance of forgiveness	Discusses feeding the soul, guarding the heart, and daily choices.

Forgiveness is more than a moment; it's a lifestyle. It starts with one decision, but it must be walked out every day. The enemy would love you to think that forgiving once is enough to close the door permanently, but the truth is: some days, you must forgive again. Not because your initial act wasn't real, but because pain echoes—and freedom requires consistency. To walk in forgiveness daily means to choose release before resentment can rise again. It means you decide at the beginning of each day, "I will not be ruled by what was done to me. I will be led by what Christ did for me." This choice doesn't always come easy. Sometimes you must whisper through tears. But that's where the power of God meets your weakness. That's where grace fills the gap. Freedom is a fragile thing when it isn't kept. Just as physical healing requires rest, nourishment, and protection, spiritual healing requires intentional maintenance. What are you feeding your soul today? Who are you giving access to your heart? What thoughts are you letting replay in your mind? These are the questions that shape your walk. Walking in daily forgiveness also means taking authority over the lies. Lies like, "They don't deserve it" or "You're being weak by letting go." No, you are being like Christ. You are choosing to lay down the offense so you can rise in obedience. Each time you forgive, you grow. You make space for peace. You silence the enemy's accusations. You partner with heaven. And on the days when you feel like you can't do it, remember: Jesus didn't just die so you could forgive once. He died so that forgiveness could become your nature—your rhythm, your weapon, your freedom. Forgiveness doesn't mean reconciliation in every case, but it does mean release. It means you no longer carry what you were never meant to. You walk lighter. You breathe easier. You love deeper. Today, take the next step. Walk in forgiveness. Speak it. Declare it. Pray through it. And know that with each step, chains are falling—not just around you, but through you, for others too.

WHAT FORGIVENESS IS NOT

To forgive is not to:

- Say what happened was okay.
- Pretend it didn't hurt.
- Reconciliating with someone is still harmful.
- Forget what happened.

Forgiveness is not a feeling, it's a choice. A continual one. It's the act of releasing your right to revenge, so that God can bring justice His way—and so that you don't stay stuck in cycles of bitterness and blame.

"Do not take revenge... but leave room for God's wrath."
— ROMANS 12:19

TESTIMONY: RESTORING HER IDENTITY AFTER HIDDEN BURNOUT

Her Story: She was the dependable one—the "yes" woman, the volunteer, the one who never said she was tired. Church events, family gatherings, work projects—she was there, serving, fixing, making sure everyone else was okay. On the outside, it was faithfulness. Inside, it was silent exhaustion and fear of disappointing people. She believed her worth came from being needed, and slowing down felt like failing God. But one day, after serving at yet another event, she went home, closed the door, and collapsed in tears she had held back for years. The weight of unspoken expectations, people's opinions, and the fear of letting others down had become too heavy. She realized she no longer knew who she was without a role to fill or a need to meet. Regret whispered, "You wasted your life trying to please everyone." She felt like she had nothing left to give and no clear sense of who God created her to be. In that quiet, broken moment, she prayed, "God, I don't know how to live differently, but I want to." That prayer became the seed of restoration. She stepped back from commitments, risking people's disappointment to find God's voice again. She began counseling to untangle her identity from the fear of rejection. She spent quiet mornings with God, not to prepare for another assignment, but to be loved. She journaled her feelings instead of suppressing them. Slowly, God began to reveal that her value was never in her performance but in being His daughter. She learned to say "no" without guilt and "yes" only when God led. Joy, which had long been absent, returned in small, unexpected ways: laughing without anxiety, resting without shame, serving with genuine love instead of pressure. She realized restoration didn't mean returning to the busyness; it meant rebuilding her life around God's priorities, not people's demands. She learned that pleasing God sometimes meant disappointing people—and that was okay. Now, she smiles without regret, living with open hands, knowing her worth is secure in Christ. Restoration became her testimony, proving that even years of hidden burnout and people-pleasing can be redeemed, and that you can live a life of peace, purpose, and freedom again.

TESTIMONY: FORGIVING A FATHER WHO WAS NEVER THERE

His Story: He grew up angry—at the world, at himself, and especially at the man who gave him life but not love.

His father's absence became the wound he carried into every relationship.

He said he had "moved on," but deep down, he judged every man through that filter of pain.

And it started to show up in how he fathered his own children—distant, distracted, guarded.

In counseling, he was challenged: "What would forgiveness look like, even if your father never apologizes?"

That question broke him. Because it revealed something powerful:

Forgiveness isn't about what they do, it's about what you release.

He wrote his father a letter he never mailed.

He let the pain come to the surface—then he let it go.

And in doing so, he became the kind of father he never had.

The Power of Letting Go is so rewarding and brings healing. Always remember that forgiveness is not weakness. It's warfare. When you forgive, you dismantle the enemy's favorite stronghold—offense.

Unforgiveness says:

"You owe me."
"Need closure."
"Can't move on until they make it right."

But forgiveness says:

"Trust God to restore what I cannot recover."
"No longer tethered to the one who hurt me."
"Release this, so it won't define me."

And when you let go—really let go—your soul exhales.

FORGIVING YOURSELF

One of the hardest people to forgive is often... you.
What about the mistakes you made in pain?

____

____

____

____

____

The people you hurt when you were trying to survive.

____

____

____

____

____

____

The times you ignored your own voice, chose the wrong path, or stayed too long?

____

____

____

____

____

____

You can't move forward while punishing yourself for where you've been.

"There is now no condemnation for those who are in Christ Jesus."
— ROMANS 8:1

God doesn't rehearse your failures. He redeems them.

A PRAYER OF FORGIVENESS

Father,

Bring you, my wounds. Bring you the betrayal, the abandonment, the offenses—spoken and unspoken.

Release every person who has hurt me. Choose to forgive—not because they deserve it, but because I need to be free.

Cancel the debt I've been holding against them.

Let go of bitterness and judgment.
Open my hands to receive peace.
I also choose to forgive myself.
Renounce shame, regret, and self-blame.
You are the Judge. You are the Healer. You are the One who restores.
Trust you to deal with justice in Your timing. Trust you to rebuild what was broken.
In Jesus' name, Amen.

Ask yourself:

1. Who do I need to release, whether they ever apologize or not?

____

____

____

____

____

____

2. What weight am I carrying that God wants me to put down?

____

____

____

____

____

____

3. Where do I need to forgive myself to fully walk in freedom?

____

____

____

____

____

____

Journaling:

"God, I am ready to release. Carried this pain for too long. Help me surrender it completely and walk in forgiveness—one day at a time."

____

____

____

____

____

____

____

____

____

____

____

____

____

____

____

____

____

____

____

____

____

____

____
____
____
____
____
____
____
____
____
____
____
____
____
____
____

FINAL DECLARATION: Forgiven; therefore, I choose to forgive others. I don't forgive for closure or reconciliation, but FOR FREEDOM.

CHAPTER 6: SOUL REPAIR
MORE THAN SURFACE HEALING

"He Restores My Soul..."— PSALM 23:3

"He has sent me to bind up the brokenhearted... to comfort all who mourn... to bestow on them a crown of beauty instead of ashes..."
— ISAIAH 61:1–3

Some wounds go beyond the body. They go beyond what others can see. They settle in your soul—the part of you that thinks, feels, hopes, fears, and remembers. Soul wounds are slow. Soul wounds are subtle, but heavy. They don't always scream. Sometimes, they whisper:

Sometimes, they whisper:

> *"You're still broken."*
> *"Nothing's really changed."*
> *"Don't trust too quickly."*
> *"You're still broken."*
> *"Nothing's really changed."*
> *"Don't trust too quickly."*
> *"You're too damaged to be whole again."*

Soul wounds can develop through deep disappointment, traumatic loss, chronic stress, betrayal, childhood pain, or long-term neglect. Because they're invisible, we often function through them—until we reach the point where we can't; that's when God, our Shepherd, steps in. Not to patch you up, but to restore your soul. God will heal you from the inside out. We often pray for God to fix external things—broken relationships, finances, jobs, opportunities—but true soul repair begins within. The soul carries the silent burdens: the ache you don't speak about, the disappointments you minimize, the fears you try to escape, the broken places no one sees. These whispers may sound like your own voice. They often hide behind busyness, distractions, accomplishments, or even religious activity. You can lead, serve, perform—and still bleed inside. Not every soul wound result from a single traumatic event, some come from a lifetime of silent erosion. Death by a thousand disappointments. Pain left unaddressed. Emotions bottled up. Secrets buried too deep to reach. Soul wounds form through deep disappointment, betrayal, rejection, trauma, grief, abuse, neglect, abandonment, or long-term emotional exhaustion. They can even stem from unmet expectations—when you prayed and God seemed silent... when you trusted someone and they walked away... when life veered in a direction you didn't expect. And because they're invisible, we often function through them—until we reach our breaking point.

We learn how to smile and still be numb.
We know how to say "I'm good" when we're barely holding it together.
We learn to suppress instead of healing.
To perform instead of process.
To avoid instead of confronting.

But eventually, the pain we refuse to face begins to control us. We hit emotional walls, burn out, break down, lash out, and isolate ourselves. In those moments, our coping mechanisms crumble under the weight of what our soul has carried for too long.

That's when the Shepherd steps in.
Psalm 23:3 says, "He restores my soul."
Not: "He patches it up."
Not: "He tells me to tough it out."
Not: "He says get over it."
No... He restores it.

The Hebrew word for "restore" means to bring something back to its original condition. It means to refresh, to repair, to make whole again. That's what God does. He doesn't just fix you so you can keep functioning—He heals you so you can start flourishing. When you let Him. Because soul restoration isn't surface work, it's a deep work. It's God meeting you where no one else can go. The places are too fragile to touch. The moments are too painful to speak of. The memories you buried because you didn't know what else to do with them. You may be wondering, how does He do it? What does soul restoration even look like?

It begins with presence.
Psalm 23 begins with:
"The Lord is my Shepherd; I shall not want."

Everything starts from that. His presence is the foundation. God doesn't rush into your pain with answers—He enters it with compassion. He is close to the brokenhearted. He doesn't flinch at your raw emotions or step back when you mention the things you've tried to forget. He walks with you, not just to lead you send, but to bring you back—back to the moments that shaped you, so He can begin to reshape you. Soul restoration also involves truth. Healing starts when God's truth replaces the lies that pain has planted in you. You've believed, "I'm not enough." Or "I'll never be free." Or "What happened to me defines me." But God speaks a better word.

He says:

"You are fearfully and wonderfully made."- (PSALM 139:14)

"You are chosen, not forsaken."- (1 PETER 2:9)

"You are being renewed day by day."- (2 CORINTHIANS 4:16)

The lies that come from your wounds are not the final word in your life. The Shepherd restores your soul by telling you who you truly are— and who you've always been to Him. Then comes the hardest part: letting go. Soul healing often requires release. Releasing bitterness. Releasing guilt. Releasing the pressure to be okay all the time. Releasing the need to have all the answers. Releasing the belief that healing means forgetting. It doesn't. Healing doesn't erase your story, it redeems it. God is not asking you to ignore your pain. He's inviting you to give Him access to it. That's where healing begins. Not in pretending to be whole, but in giving God the broken pieces you've been holding together on your own.

You've prayed for God to fix what's around you—your relationships, your finances, your job, your circumstances. But soul restoration doesn't begin on the outside. It starts within. It begins when you stop hiding and start giving Him what hurts. You don't have to be strong for God to restore you. You just must be willing. Willing to sit still long enough for Him to speak. Willing to revisit the pain without reliving the shame. Willing to believe that your soul can be whole again—even if you've lived in pieces for a long time.

"He restores my soul."
That's not just a versus a promise.
Not just poetic—personal.

Right now, wherever you are on your journey, whether you're limping from something recent or still bleeding from something years ago—your Shepherd sees you. He knows what you've hidden. He knows what you've carried. He understands the weight of wounds that don't show on the outside. And He's not afraid of your pain. He's not finished with your story. Let Him in. Allow Him to restore what life tried to take. Let Him bring beauty from broken places. Allow Him to remind you of who you are—beneath the pain, beyond the fear, behind the mask.

You are not too far gone.
You are not too broken.
You are not too late.
You are not alone.

God's restoration doesn't happen all at once. It's not a quick fix—it's a sacred process. Sometimes it occurs in quiet moments of prayer; sometimes through godly counsel or spiritual community; other times through tears you didn't realize you still needed to cry. But always, God's goal is wholeness. Wholeness is different from perfection. It doesn't mean you'll never feel pain again. It doesn't mean you'll never remember what hurt you. It means the pain no longer controls you. It means the memory no longer defines you. It means you can walk through life without the limp of shame or the weight of unspoken grief. God is patient with your process. He's not in a hurry to rush your healing. That's hard for us sometimes, especially when we feel pressure to move on or "be better already." But the Shepherd is gentle. He doesn't drag you send. He leads you with kindness. He meets you right where you are and walks with you step by step. Some days, restoration looks like it is still choosing to rest instead of running. Other days, it looks like courage—choosing to speak rather than suppress. And some days, it simply looks like surrender—saying, "God, I can't carry this anymore... but You can." That's where the soul finds relief. In surrender. In honesty. In safety of His presence. When David said, "He restores my soul," it was a declaration of trust. David had been through valleys. He had made mistakes. He had known sorrow, betrayal, loss, and regret. And still, he spoke with confidence: God restores. That word wasn't rooted in dreaming—it was rooted in experience. God doesn't just restore ideal people with perfect resumes. He restores the wounded. The weary. The ones who've walked through fire feel like they have nothing left to offer. He restores people like David. People like you. People like me. You don't need to have it all together for God to begin.

You just need to be open.
Open to His voice.

Open to His timing.
Open to being loved in the places you feel unlovable.

Restoration often starts with vulnerability. That's why the enemy works hard to keep you silent, guarded, and ashamed. But healing can't happen in hiding. We're only as whole as we are honest. And God can only heal the real version of you— not the pretend one. The broken, beautiful, complicated, tired, hopeful you. You might wonder, 'But what if I go back to those places and fall apart again?'

Here's the truth: sometimes falling apart is the beginning of falling into grace.

There's something sacred about being broken in the hands of the One who knows how to restore you. He is the Potter. You are the clay. And when He restores, He doesn't rebuild you as you were—He remakes you into something even stronger. Even more beautiful. Even more whole. Isaiah 61:3 says He gives "a crown of beauty instead of ashes, the oil of joy instead of mourning, and a garment of praise instead of a spirit of despair." That is the God you serve. A God who exchanges the wreckage of what was for the restoration of what will be. But here's the thing about restoration, it's not just about you. When God heals your soul, your healing becomes hope for someone else. Your testimony becomes someone else's survival story. Your scars become signs that healing is real, possible, and near. That's why the enemy fights soul healing so fiercely. Because a restored soul doesn't just survive—it shines. And that light pushes back the darkness in others. So, take the journey. Trust the Shepherd. You don't have to understand every step. You just must take the next one. And then the next one. And then the one after that. Little by little, grace by grace, your soul will rise again.

You will not always feel like this.
You will not always carry this.
You will not always be stuck in what was.
The Shepherd is still leading.
The Healer is still working.
The Restorer is still restoring.

Let Him finish what He started in you.
You are not behind. You are becoming.
You are not broken beyond repair. You are being rebuilt.
You are not forgotten. You are held.

TESTIMONY: CHILDHOOD TRAUMA

Her Story: She didn't think her childhood was traumatic. There was no violence. No scandal. Just silence. Distance. Disconnection. But that absence of affection shaped how she loved it.

She always believed she had to earn love or remain invisible to maintain peace. It wasn't until a counselor asked her, "When did you first start hiding who you were?" that something shifted. She traced it back to when she was five, overhearing a parent say, "She's too emotional." From that moment, she closed her heart. Her healing didn't happen all at once; it came in layers—as she invited God into the memories she had avoided.

And slowly, the five-year-old inside her began to feel safe again.

And in His time, and in His hands, your soul will be whole again.

He restores my soul.

It's more than a line in a Psalm.

It's your promise.

It's your path.

It's your future.

"Above all else, guard your heart, for everything you do flows from it."
— PROVERBS 4:23

Your heart is not just your emotions—it's the center of your being.

And God doesn't want to just protect it. He wants to repair it.

That means healing the:

- Memories that still sting.
- Words that still echo.
- Patterns that still repeat.

TESTIMONY: WHEN NUMB WAS NORMAL

His Story: He didn't think anything was wrong. Chris was the dependable one. The strong one. The one everyone called when they needed help. He kept busy with work, church projects, and weekend plans. Staying busy kept the feelings away—or so he thought. But deep down, numb had become his normal. He couldn't remember the last time he really felt joy... or sorrow... or anything in between. Trivial things started setting him off—unexpected anger, sudden sadness, waves of anxiety that came out of nowhere. It all came to a head one Sunday morning. Sitting in the church parking lot, Chris couldn't bring himself to go inside. For the first time, he whispered words he'd avoided for years: "God... I'm not okay." At that moment something cracked open. Through counseling, prayer, and honest conversations with friends, Chris realized what he'd been carrying: years of suppressed pain from childhood rejection, emotional neglect, and the pressure to always "hold it together." God didn't rush his healing. He walked with Chris— patiently, gently, layer by layer. The process wasn't pretty. Some days felt like progress; others wanted to start over. But little by little, Chris learned how to feel again... how to trust again... how to breathe again. And for the first time in a long time, he's starting to believe: "Maybe I really can be whole again."

THE PROCESS OF SOUL REPAIR

1. Name the Pain

You can't heal what you won't name. Denial delays healing.
Ask: Where am I still bleeding internally?

2. Grieve Honestly

Grief is a gift. It means you're still tender.
Let the tears come. Write the letter. Sit with the memory.
You don't stay there—but you visit so God can enter.

3. Invite God into the Memory

Healing isn't about erasing what happened.
It's about letting God redefine it. Ask Him:
"Where were You when this happened?"
Often, He'll show you the comfort, the protection, or the truth you missed.

4. Break Inner Vows

Sometimes, pain causes us to make silent promises:
"I'll never trust again."
"Won't let anyone get close."
"I don't need anyone."
These vows protect us for a time—but imprison us overall.
Break them and replace them with truth.

A Prayer for Soul Healing

Lord,
Give You permission to go deeper.
Not just into what I show others—but into what I've hidden.
Heal the memories I've buried.
Touch the places I stopped believing You could restore.
Break the lies I've lived with for so long, I've called them normal.
Break the cycles. Break the fear.
Restore my soul—not just the symptoms, but the source.
Fill me with peace where there was anxiety.
With joy there was numbness.
With wholeness where there was fragmentation.
Surrender every layer of my inner world to You.

And I trust that what You rebuild will be more beautiful than what was broken.

In Jesus' name, Amen.

Ask Yourself:

1. What painful memory do I still carry in silence?

____

____

____

____

____

____

2. Have I truly grieved my losses, or have I rushed past them?

____

____

____

____

____

____

3. What silent vows or inner beliefs are keeping me guarded?

____

____

____

____

____

____

Journaling:

"God, the part of my soul that still hurts is..."
"This is the truth I need to believe instead..."

"This is the lie I'm ready to release..."
Elaborate on the phrases and ask for God's response to you.

____

____

____

____

____

____

____

____

____

____

____

____

____

____

____

____

____

____

____

____

____

____

____

FINAL DECLARATION: God is restoring my soul from the inside out. I release what has wounded me and receive His healing. Wholeness, peace, and renewal belong to me through Him.

CHAPTER 7: RESTORATION WITHOUT REGRET

BEYOND THE WRECKAGE: BUILDING WITHOUT LOOKING BACK

"Will restore to you the years that the swarming locust has eaten..."
— JOEL 2:25

"And we know that all things work together for good to those who love God..."
— ROMANS 8:28

Regret is a thief.

It doesn't always show up loudly. Sometimes it tiptoes in quietly, late at night, when your mind replays conversations that cannot be redone and moments that cannot be retrieved. Other times, regret rushes in like a wave—unexpected and overwhelming—triggered by a song, a memory, or even the anniversary date of something you would rather forget. It comes to remind you of your missteps, your bad choices, and your moments of weakness. It points an accusing finger at your past and whispers, "If only you had done things differently." Regret is relentless. It will rehearse the scene again until you're no longer looking toward your future, you're staring at the wreckage of what was, wishing for a rewind button that doesn't exist. But here's the truth: God is not the author of regret. He is the Author of redemption. Redemption is His specialty. Where regret tells you that you ruined it, God reminds you that He can rebuild it. Where regret insists that you missed your chance, God says He is making all things new. Restoration doesn't require you to forget what happened, but it does invite you to stop living there emotionally and mentally. You were never meant to build your life around what broke you. You were meant to build forward—with hope, with healing, and with the assurance that God can do more with what remains than you ever imagined. Restoration is not God pretending that nothing happened. It is His way of proving that nothing you've been through will be wasted. He will use the heartbreak you endured. He will redeem the detour you took. He will even work through the worst decision you ever made to bring about His purpose in your life.

Joel 2:25 gives us this promise: "I will restore to you the years the locusts have eaten." Notice that it doesn't say God will give you the same years back as though nothing ever happened. It says He will restore those years. God doesn't rewind time, but He does redeem it in ways only He can.I f you have been through divorce, failure, addiction, betrayal, loss, or seasons marked by shame, you probably know the voices that come with regret all too well. You have heard whispers that say, "You're disqualified now," or "You blew your chance." You've carried the belief that you will never recover from this, that everyone will remember what you did, and that moving on is impossible. But here's the truth that God wants to remind you today: Restoration silences those lies. God does not consult your past when planning your future. He does not hold you hostage to previous chapters of your story. Instead, He looks at your heart right now—this very moment. He is not focused on the chapter you wish you could erase; He is focused on the surrender you offer Him today. God does not require your perfection to begin the work of restoration. What He asks for is your permission. He wants your permission to step into the broken places and begin mending what feels unfixable. He wants your permission to tell truth over the lies that regret has been feeding you for far too long. He wants your permission to lead you into new beginnings, even if you don't feel ready or worthy. Restoration begins when you stop hiding the wreckage and start handing it to God. It may feel safer to pretend you're fine—to stay busy, keep smiling, and convince yourself you've moved on. But healing never happens through avoidance. Restoration doesn't come to those who fake wholeness. It comes to those who are honest enough to say, "God, I'm still hurting here." You don't have to unpack your past with everyone, but you do need to bring it to God. Only He knows how to rebuild without leaving you stuck in regret. Sometimes the hardest part of restoration isn't believing that God can do it; it's believing that you're worthy of receiving it. Guilt will tell you that restoration is reserved for people who messed up less than you did. Shame will convince you that moving forward means you're ignoring the damage you caused. But grace speaks louder than both. Grace says, "Yes, you messed up—but My mercy is greater." Grace reminds you, "Yes, there were consequences—but I'm not done with you yet." Grace declares, "You are still called, still loved, and still chosen." Let me remind you: Some of the most powerful stories in the Bible came from people who knew failure intimately. Peter denied Jesus three times, and still, Jesus called him to help build the Church. David fell into sin, yet God still called him a man after His own heart. Paul persecuted Christians, yet God trusted him to write most of the New Testament. Why did God continue to use them? Because restoration doesn't erase the past—it redeems it. God doesn't waste anything that is surrendered to Him. He will use your tears, your sleepless nights, and even the years you feel were lost.

You may not regain the exact moments or relationships you once had, but you will gain something even better: peace that calms your heart, freedom that lifts your burdens, and purpose that fuels your steps forward. God will give you a future no longer bound by what you've done or what has been done to you. Sometimes, restoration means rebuilding the same relationship but with stronger foundations and healthier communication. Other times, it wants to create something entirely new because, honestly, your healing needs a fresh start. Restoration can also be about reclaiming your identity after years of believing lies about who you are. And often, it's simply waking up with hope again—hope that tomorrow can look different than yesterday. You can't change the past, but you can stop dragging it into your present. You don't have to keep replaying the wreckage. You don't have to keep apologizing for just existing. You don't have to carry the weight of shame. God's invitation to you is clear and straightforward: "Let Me restore you." Restoration doesn't mean you will forget what happened. It means you will look back and see God's grace covering the places where guilt once lived. You will remember the pain but also feel peace. You will recall the failure, but sense freedom. You will see the wreckage but no longer live there. Restoration without regret means learning from the past without staying in it. It means you will hold onto your testimony without clutching the trauma. It means you will move forward—not as punishment for your mistakes, but as evidence of God's mercy at work in your life. You've been hesitant to dream again. Part of you feels like dreaming is risky. Wanting more after what happened seems irresponsible or naive. But listen: It is okay to start rebuilding again. It is OK to hope again. It is OK to smile without guilt. It is OK to accept joy without questioning if you deserve it. You are not your past. You are not your failures. You are not the sum of your regrets. You are a living, breathing example of redemption in progress. If the enemy cannot destroy you with what happened, he will try to paralyze you with regret. But you don't have to let him. Today, you can choose restoration. You can decide to move forward. You can choose healing. You don't need to understand how God will do it—you just must let Him. You may feel like the wreckage defines you now, but give it time— and most importantly, give it to God—and someday, you'll look back and realize: "This was the place where God rebuilt me." God will not restore you despite your mistakes. He will restore you right in the middle of them. Because where regret says, "You're done," restoration boldly declares, "You're just getting started."

You may wonder how to live out restoration when the wreckage feels louder than the promise, but it begins with shifting your posture from striving to surrendering. Restoration is not a destination you reach through your own strength; it is a daily partnership with God, choosing to let Him lead your rebuilding one step at a time, trusting that He restores your soul even when your circumstances haven't changed yet (Psalm 23:3). Regret keeps you stuck in guilt, but God invites you to reframe regret into reflection so you can grow in wisdom instead of staying in shame, asking yourself what you've learned about God's character, how your pain revealed areas needing healing, and how your story can help others find hope. Restoration is rarely instant and often unfolds in layers, requiring you to embrace the process without expecting perfection, remembering that He who began a decent work in you will complete it (Philippians 1:6). Some days you'll feel strong, and others fragile, but you're not required to fake strength you don't have; you only need to keep showing up as God mends your heart step by step, whether it's reaching out for counseling, forgiving yourself, or releasing shame that has weighed you down for too long. Renewal of your mindset involves releasing the regret of relationship outcomes—words you wish you could take back or painful endings. And while this new outlook doesn't always mean every relationship will return to what it once was, it does mean your heart can be healed regardless of others' choices, as you live at peace, as far as it depends on you (Romans 12:18). As God restores you, you may find yourself smiling, hoping, and dreaming again, and regret may try to make you feel guilty for embracing joy, but you must remember restoration is not a betrayal of your past; it is the fruit of God's mercy and evidence of His new thing in your life (Isaiah 43:18-19). Stop apologizing for your healing. Live restored without explaining your joy, without dragging your past into your present, and without shrinking under shame, trusting that you are not erasing your story but allowing God to redeem it fully. Today, you have a choice: to stay in the wreckage or to hand it to God and begin rebuilding with Him, letting His restoration refine you rather than letting regret define you. You may not know what the future holds, but you can trust the One who holds it, and you do not have to fear restoration because it is not here to punish you but to propel you into the fullness of God's promises. Let go of guilt, release shame, and open your heart to the possibility that God can create beauty from the ashes you thought would bury you, because restoration without regret does not mean you will never remember what happened, but it means you will no longer allow it to control you. It means you will rise each morning with hope, go to bed with peace, walk through your days with purpose, and see yourself as God sees you—redeemed, chosen, loved, and still called. Will you let Him restore you?

Focus encourages you to develop rhythms that support your healing—taking time to rest without guilt, seeking counseling if needed, spending time in prayer and the Word, and surrounding yourself with uplifting people instead of judgmental ones. It involves celebrating small progress without disqualifying yourself because you aren't "there" yet, understanding that healing is not a race but a walk with God at your side, day by day.

As you walk in restoration, you will notice your perspective change: you will see your scars not as reminders of shame but as evidence of God's faithfulness. You will begin to thank God not just for victories but for lessons learned in the valleys that drew you closer to Him. Reflecting, you will see the places where you once felt abandoned and realize God was carrying you through the hardest moments, working behind the scenes in ways you couldn't see. Psalm 147:3 says, "He heals the brokenhearted and binds up their wounds," and you will recognize how He has been healing wounds you thought would define you forever, gently transforming your deepest regrets into your greatest testimonies.

Restoration will also reveal that your identity is not based on what you did or what was done to you but on who God says you are. You are not your past. You are not your failures. You are not your regrets. You are a child of God, fully loved, fully seen, and fully known, called to walk in freedom and hope. You no longer need to hide your story in fear of judgment; instead, you can share it in faith that God will use it to encourage others still trapped in the wreckage you once knew. Your life becomes a living testimony that it is possible to move forward without regret, to build without constantly looking back, and to live without shame overshadowing your steps. If God can restore Peter after denial, David after moral failure, and Paul after persecution, He can restore you completely, too, using your life to display His mercy and power to the world around you. Restoration without regret means you are free to build again, dream again, hope again, and live again—not pretending the pain didn't happen but proving that God's grace is bigger than the pain ever was. You don't have to wait until you feel "ready" or until everything is perfect to start living in restoration; you simply need to say, "Yes, God, I give You permission to restore me." You can breathe again, laugh again, and trust again, knowing that God is writing a new chapter that is not chained to your mistakes but anchored in His mercy. The enemy will try to remind you of your failures to keep you silent, but you can remind him of your restoration, boldly declaring that God is using your life for His glory. Today, let restoration be your declaration: that your story is not over, your past is not your prison, and your future is still full of promise because God is not finished with you yet. Moving forward in freedom means learning to live with open hands, trusting God with the outcomes that are beyond your control.

Regret often causes you to replay conversations, moments, and decisions, trying to figure out what you could have done differently. Still, God invites you to let go of the illusion that you can fix the past through overthinking. Instead, He calls you to trust that He can redeem every part of your story, even the chapters you'd like to erase. Proverbs 3:5-6 says, "Trust in the Lord with all your heart and lean not on your own understanding; in all your ways submit to Him, and He will make your paths straight." Restoration often involves surrendering what you don't understand and allowing God to lead you forward, even when you can't see how He will bring good out of it. It's choosing to stop rehearsing your failures and start rehearsing His faithfulness. It's giving yourself permission to grieve what was lost while holding onto hope that God will bring beauty from ashes, trusting that He is not finished with you yet.

TESTIMONY: BEAUTY AFTER THE BREAKDOWN

Her Story: She never thought she would fully recover from the divorce. At first, she believed she was okay. She threw herself into work, her kids, ministry, and anything that kept her from sitting still for too long. But late at night, when the house was quiet, regret would slip in like an unwelcome guest. It wasn't just regret over the marriage ending, it was regret over what she said, what she didn't say, and the years she felt she wasted trying to hold everything together. Every memory played like a movie reel she couldn't turn off. Conversations replayed. Arguments echoed. The guilt weighed heavily. There were moments when she wondered if she would ever feel like herself again—whoever that even was anymore. One night, curled up on the bedroom floor, she whispered, "God, I can't carry this anymore." That was her turning point. Little by little, God began softening the hard places in her heart. Through counseling, prayer, and vulnerable conversations with trusted friends, she started to let go of what she had been holding onto so tightly: guilt, shame, the self-blame. Healing didn't erase her story, but it did begin to redefine her identity. She realized she wasn't the sum of her mistakes. She was loved. Chosen. Redeemed. And slowly, joy started returning to her heart.

TESTIMONY: BUILDING AGAIN AFTER FAILURE

His Story: He built his entire identity around being successful. The business was growing, his social media following was increasing, and on the surface, it seemed like everything was going well. But when the business failed—unexpectedly and publicly—he felt like his entire life collapsed with it. Failure wasn't just a monetary loss; it felt deeply personal. He withdrew from friends, stopped attending church, and silenced every phone call that came through. The enemy's voice was loud during that season: "You're done. You'll never recover. This is who you are now—the guy who failed." For months, he lived in that mental space—ashamed, isolated, and stuck. But one afternoon, sitting in the back row of a Sunday service he almost didn't attend, the pastor said something that felt meant just for him: "Failure isn't your final chapter. God still writes comeback stories."

That sentence opened something up. It didn't solve everything overnight, but it was enough to give him hope again. He began rebuilding—not the business first—but himself. His faith. His relationships. His identity. Now, looking back, he realizes the failure didn't destroy him—it redirected him. What felt like the end was really God's way of clearing the ground for something healthier, deeper, and more purpose driven. He's rebuilding it again, but this time, without regret.

Prayer for Restoration Without Regret

Father, thank You that my past does not disqualify me from Your purpose.

You see the places where regret has taken root in my heart, and You meet me there with grace.

Today, I released the weight of what I cannot change. Surrender the moments I wish I could redo and the decisions I wish I could reverse.

Help me stop rehearsing the wreckage and start receiving Your restoration.

Remind me that nothing is wasted in Your hands—not my tears, not my mistakes, not my broken places.

Give me the courage to build again. To hope again. To trust You with my future.

I believe that what You restore will be stronger than what was lost.

Thank You for loving me through the process.

In Jesus' name, Amen.

Ask Yourself:

1. What regrets have you been carrying that God is inviting you to release today?

---

2. In what areas do you need to give God permission to begin restoring your heart and future?

---

3. Write down one truth from Scripture that reminds you that your story isn't over.

---

4. What new thing could God be calling you to build in this next season?

---

5. How can you start embracing restoration without dragging along shame?

____

____

____

____

____

GRACE OVER PERFECTION

Practical Steps to Walk in Grace:

1. Release the Timeline.

Let go of what "should have happened by now." Restoration is on God's clock.

2. Forgive Yourself.

Not because you were right—but because grace says you don't have to stay stuck.

3. Redefine Success.

Restoration doesn't always look like public applause. Sometimes it's private peace.

4. Speak Restoration Daily.

"God is restoring me. Past will not be my prison."

Journaling:

Close your eyes and picture...
A version of you did not define by what broke you.
A future not bound by the timeline you missed.
A life that speaks, "God did it, even from this."

Now write:

1. What have you been afraid of rebuilding?

____

____

____

____

____

____

2. What part of your story still feels heavy with regret?

____

____

____

____

____

____

3. What would your life look like if you honestly believed God could restore all things?

____

____

____

____

____

____

FINAL DECLARATION: I will no longer live in regret. God is restoring my life, my peace, and my purpose. Past will not define me—His grace will.

CHAPTER 8: WHOLENESS IN PURPOSE

HEALING WITH PURPOSE IN MIND: TRANSITIONING FOR THE NEXT ASSIGNMENT

Healing is a beautiful and necessary part of the journey, but it was never meant to be the destination. Many of us have spent seasons of our lives crying out to God for healing—whether from emotional wounds, mental struggles, spiritual confusion, or physical pain. When healing finally arrives, or even when the process starts, it feels like stepping into the light after sitting in darkness for too long. But God's intention was never for us to heal just so we could admire it and stay where we are. His plan has always been for us to walk into our next assignment, equipped and ready for the purpose He designed for us before we were born. The Apostle Paul reminds us in Ephesians 2:10 that we are God's masterpiece. He created us anew in Christ Jesus so we could do the good works He planned for us long ago. This means your purpose was set long before your pain appeared. Your healing isn't about fixing what broke; it's about preparing you to walk in what God has called you to do. Your breakdown was never a detour; it was always a bridge to your assignment. We often fall into the trap of thinking we must reach some imaginary level of perfection before God can use us. We believe the lie that we need to be completely without scars, tears, or doubts. But the truth is, your healing journey doesn't disqualify you from purpose; it qualifies you in ways comfort alone never could. The voice that whispers, "You're too messed up to help others," is not God's voice. That is fear, shame, and the enemy trying to silence your testimony. Fear often disguises itself as humility, convincing you that sitting on the sidelines is noble. But God isn't asking for your perfection. He's asking for your willingness. Romans 12:2 says we are to be transformed by the renewing of our minds. This isn't just a suggestion for when we feel like it; it's a command because God knows we can't walk in our calling if we're too wounded or distracted to recognize it. The healing of the mind often marks the start of the journey to purpose. Before you fully step into your assignment, God will change how you see yourself. He'll renew your perspective on your value, worth, and ability to impact others for His glory. For many of us, this season isn't about healing; it's about transition. Transition can be difficult because it means letting go of one thing and stepping into something new. The word "retire" holds special significance here. To retire means to leave one role or form of expression and move into the next phase. Breaking it down further, "tire" reflects both fatigue and growth. Sometimes it means growing weary, signaling the need for rest.

Other times, it reflects the natural cycle of maturation and expanding into new areas. God is saying to many of us, "It's time to rest from one form of expression and move into the next." He's shifting you from physical roles of protection and authority into higher levels of spiritual influence. What once defined your daily assignments no longer aligns with where He's asking you to serve. This is a crossover season. If you're reading these words, it's not by accident. Change is coming to your life. Transformation is on the horizon. God uses every opportunity to reveal Himself and show us who He created us to be from the foundation of the world. You may not understand why certain doors closed, relationships ended, or seasons became painful, but God is about to make sense of it all. He loves you too much to leave you in confusion. This transitional season isn't meant to break you; it's meant to build you. It's both a season of transformation and an opportunity for growth. Some may think, "I need to get myself together before I can get right with God." But the truth is, none of us can "get right" on our own. That's why God sent His Son. Jesus died to conduct what we could never do through our own strength—righteousness. God is speaking a personal and specific word to you. Be prepared to worship like David did—completely lost in joy and praise, regardless of public opinion, just as he danced before the Lord when the Ark was restored. God is calling you to rejoice freely. Your worship will look different, it will be raw, unfiltered, authentic. If you didn't know before, know this now: God has been with you all these years, even when you didn't realize the spiritual battles you were facing. Nothing in your life will look familiar. People who knew the old you will struggle to recognize the latest version God is revealing. They're used to seeing you speak, walk, and react a certain way. But God is calling you out of the wilderness and into abundance.

This is a season of transition from dryness to overflow, from isolation to intimacy with the Holy Spirit. At any moment, God can use you to do the miraculous. He's already allowed you to experience His presence; now He's increasing the heat. Everything in your life, your marriage, family, ministry, or business—is about to shift. Like David, who left a legacy through land he purchased for Solomon to build on, there's a spiritual inheritance that God is releasing to you. This inheritance isn't just for you but for Joshua and many others He will send your way. This is the beginning of your spiritual fatherhood. God says, "Pour every chance you get. Pour like your life depends on it." You've laid the foundation, and now it's time to build. Parenting requires patience, but mentoring requires even more. Just as after Moses died, God told Joshua to lead the Israelites into the Promised Land. Their journey demanded faith, prayer, and total reliance on God. When they faced the Red Sea, they had to wait for His instruction. Your next steps will come from God alone. This is a season when He will quiet the noise to get your attention. Healing and wholeness must happen before you cross over. The outdated version of you can't enter the new place God is leading you. Just like the generation that left Egypt and died in the wilderness, certain mindsets, and behaviors in you must die. God told Joshua, "I will be with you just as I was with Moses." That same promise is for you: "I was with you before, and I will be with you now." And what's ahead will be greater than what you've known. You've been through too much to stay the same. You've learned valuable lessons, and now God is teaching you how to apply them. The key to your future is obedience. Joshua 5:8 reminds us that after all the males were circumcised, they rested until they healed. Rest is part of the process. God is bringing you into divine rest—a place of complete trust and dependence on Him. This season, nothing else will matter but what He says. You won't feel restless while waiting. God is removing the shame of your past and bringing you into promise. Joshua and the Israelites won the victory at Jericho because they followed God's instructions perfectly. Victory comes through obedience. God is asking you to let go of what you've been holding onto. Like Achan in Joshua 7, hidden things must now be exposed and surrendered. Whatever you don't lay on the altar can destroy you and those connected to you.

The Israelites learned this the hard way when their sin affected the whole nation. What you refuse to deal with in your will may end up destroying your destiny. Even when they faced Ai, Israel saw victory when they did things God's way. The land God promised is still yours, but you must possess it. In Joshua 13:6, God told Joshua, "I Myself will drive them out." This is God's fight, but He needs your faith. Some of you wonder why others seem to prosper while you stay still. But remember, just as the tribe of Levi received no land because the Lord was their inheritance, God is saying to you, "I am your portion." Caleb, in Joshua 14, waited patiently and then boldly asked for his mountain. He didn't let fear, age, or delay keep him from pursuing what God promised. God has not forgotten His word to you. The real question is, have you forgotten what He said? Are you willing to pursue it even if the obstacles look high and the competitors seem strong? Don't settle for less out of fear—like the descendants of Manasseh who refused to drive out the Canaanites. If God said it's yours, He has already given you power over every obstacle. Even when the Canaanites had iron chariots, God told His people, "You will drive them out." (Joshua 17:18) There's still unclaimed territory in your life. God asks you the same question Joshua asked: "How long will you wait before taking possession of what I've already given you?" (Joshua 18:3). Now is the time to step out. As the land is mapped out, the people brought descriptions back to Joshua, who distributed it as God commanded. God is releasing what He promised. More than land, He's releasing Himself. When you realize that He is the promise, your heart will turn toward deeper intimacy with Him. Everything God has spoken over your life is happening. Joshua 21:45 reminds us that none of the Lord's good promises to Israel failed. Everything He spoke was fulfilled. God is declaring that you have already won. But you must remove every idol—the false things you have placed above Him. Worship God and watch Him defend you. Your idols cannot save you. The Israelites did evil in the Lord's sight and were handed over to their enemies because of it. But when Gideon tore down the altar of Baal, God moved. God doesn't have to prove Himself to you, but often He will, because of His love. What have you been asking Him for lately? This is your season of transformation. This is your crossover moment. Healing was just the start. Now it's time to walk with purpose.

The key to walking in wholeness is not waiting to "feel ready"—it's moving while still becoming.

STEPS TO EMBRACE PURPOSE:

1. Stop Disqualifying Yourself.

Your past doesn't cancel your call. It confirms your need for Christ.

2. Start Where You Are.

Purpose isn't a spotlight. It's a lifestyle. Start serving, showing up, speaking up—wherever you are.

3. Seek Alignment, Not Applause.

Your wholeness isn't proven by how people praise you, but by how you quietly and consistently obey God.

4. Write the Vision.

Take the time to name your calling—even if it scares you. Please write it down (Habakkuk 2:2).

TESTIMONY: WHEN PURPOSE FINDS YOU IN PIECES

Her Story: Healing meant returning to who I was before everything fell apart. For years, I prayed for God to take away the pain—the lingering effects of heartbreak, disappointment, betrayal, and seasons where my faith felt fragile. I just wanted peace. I wanted stability. I longed to breathe freely without the weight of anxiety pressing on my chest. But what I didn't realize was that healing isn't about going back; it's about becoming something new. This season of transition caught me off guard. I had finally reached a point where the tears weren't daily, the panic wasn't constant, and bitterness wasn't taking over. I thought that was the finish line. But God made it clear: healing was just the beginning.

I felt this nudge in my spirit—a restlessness saying, "There's more." I couldn't ignore it. Sermons began speaking directly to me. Scriptures jumped off the page. Conversations with friends turned into divine confirmations.

God wasn't just asking me to heal; He was calling me to move.

Move into uncomfortable places.

Move into rooms where my voice was needed. Move into roles where my story would become someone else's survival guide. At first, I felt disqualified. The same insecurities that haunted me before started resurfacing: "Who are you to lead? Who would listen to you? You're still figuring things out yourself." But God silenced those lies with His truth. Romans 12:2 became my anthem. Transformation by renewing my mind wasn't a one-time event; it became a daily choice. Each morning, I chose to see myself as God saw me. I had to let go of the version of myself that felt stuck in survival mode. I began stepping out in faith. I led small prayer groups and started mentoring younger women facing challenges I knew all too well. God began using my "messy middle" moments—

those times when I was still healing but willing—to minister to others. One decisive moment came when I sat with a young woman who was right where I had been just a few years earlier—confused, angry at God, questioning her worth. As I shared my story, I saw her walls come down. In that moment, God whispered to my heart, "This is why I healed you." The more I poured out, the more God poured back into me. Transition hasn't been easy. Some days I still wrestle with doubt, and some moments still trigger old wounds. But now I recognize those moments as opportunities for God to show Himself strong in my weakness. I'm learning that transition feels like grief and growth at the same time. It's grieving who you used to be while embracing who God is shaping you to be.

It's leaving the wilderness and stepping into the unknown with trembling hands but steady faith. I'm no longer afraid of unfamiliarity. I'm no longer waiting to feel "ready." God has given me spiritual territory to claim—promises to pursue, people to pour into, and a legacy to build. I realize now that my story was never about me. Healing was the key to someone else's breakthrough. Transition was the doorway to my assignment. And my obedience is the foundation for the next generation that will follow me. I may have started this journey wounded, but I'm walking into my purpose willing—and God is meeting me every step of the way.

TESTIMONY: THE WEIGHT OF TRANSITION—LEARNING TO LEAD AFTER WILDERNESS

His Story: I never expected this transition to feel like that. For years, I carried a sense of duty that became my identity. Provider, the protector, the one people called when things fell apart. I wore that role like armor. On the outside, I was respected in my community, dependable in my family, and committed to my faith. But inside, something was shifting, and I didn't know how to explain it. There was a season when exhaustion became my new regular. The responsibilities that once fueled me began to drain me. Started to wonder if I had lost my edge or if I was burnt out. I felt God pulling at me, but I didn't know what He was drawing me toward. All I knew was that I couldn't keep living the same way. At first, I called it fatigue. Then I blamed age. Eventually, I realized this was more than tiredness; it was a spiritual transition. God began to speak to me about the meaning of "retire." Not just leaving a job but retiring from one form of service to be repositioned for another. God showed me that where I once stood as a physical protector and provider, He was now calling me into a role of spiritual leadership, mentorship, and legacy building. This was a complex concept for me to accept. Used to being hands-on, solving problems, and getting things done naturally. Shifting into a spiritual assignment felt unfamiliar and, honestly, uncomfortable. But God was clear: This was my crossover.

I started studying the story of Joshua. After Moses died, God entrusted Joshua with leading the people into the Promised Land. Joshua had spent years working behind the scenes, fighting battles for others, and learning in the wilderness. But now, it was his time to step forward. God wasn't just calling him to be a fighter—He was calling him to be a leader. I could relate. God showed me that while I had spent years fighting battles in the natural—working hard, protecting my family, sacrificing myself for others—I am now being called to fight spiritual battles, to invest in others, and to leave a legacy rooted in spiritual inheritance rather than material success. One morning, during prayer, I heard God say, "Pour like your life depends on it." That hit me hard. I'd always seen pouring into others as optional—something you do when you have extra time or energy. But God made it clear: this next assignment was non-negotiable. He brought specific people into my life who needed what I carried—young men trying to find their way, families in crisis, people silently battling issues I had already overcome. God began showing me that the fights I endured weren't about my survival—they were about equipping others for their own battles. Couldn't hold back anymore. There were moments when I wondered if I was qualified for this new role. I had my own wounds. I still face times when the weight of responsibility felt overwhelming. But every time I doubted, God reminded me how He had been with me in past battles. Just like God told Joshua, "As I was with Moses, I will be with you," God told me, "As I was with you in your former seasons, I will be with you in this new one."

The transition wasn't about leaving something behind; it was about stepping into what God had always intended for me. There were battles I fought in secret that became training ground for the public assignments God was now giving me. This new season has stretched me, but it has also awakened me. I'm learning that leadership in the Kingdom isn't about title or applause, it's about obedience, legacy, and serving others even when it costs you something. God is shifting me from fighting for survival to fighting for destiny—not just mine, but for the next generation behind me.

The wilderness built my endurance.
The healing restored my heart.
Now the assignment demands my obedience.
And with God's help, I'm answering the call.

Prayer for Purpose and Wholeness

Lord God,
Thank You that I am healed and called.
Surrender the lie that says I must be perfect to be used by You.
Confess my fear, my hesitation, and the times I've disqualified myself.
Renew my mind. Reignite my vision.
Show me how to walk in the purpose You wrote over my life before I was even born.
What broke me will now help build someone else.
Use my pain as a platform. Use my healing as a guiding light.
Yours—for Your glory and the freedom of others.
In Jesus' name, Amen.

Ask Yourself:

1. What has God healed or is healing in you right now?
This is not just about your preparation for someone else.

____

____

____

____

____

2. What lie has held you back from stepping into purpose?
Write the lie. Then write the truth next to it.

____

____

____

____

____

____

3. What do you feel stirred to do—even if you don't know how yet?
That stirring could be the start of your calling.

____

____

____

____

____

Journaling:

____

____

____

____

____

____

____

____

____

____

____

____

____

____

FINAL DECLARATION: Healing Has Purpose

Today, I declare that I am not who I used to be.

I am headed, I am whole, and I am walking in the purpose God ordained for me before the foundations of the world.

Every tear I cried, every battle I fought, and every valley I walked through were preparing me for this moment.

I release the shame of my past. Surrender every hidden hurt and secret struggle to Jesus's feet.

I will not stay stuck in survival mode. I will transition with grace. I will embrace the new season God is calling me into.

My mind is being renewed. My heart is being restored. My spirit is being strengthened for the assignment ahead.

I will not fear the unfamiliar. I will not resist stretching. I will not retreat from my calling.

I receive divine rest, divine guidance, and divine courage.

What God has for me, I will possess.
What God has promised me, I will pursue.
What God has spoken over me, I will believe.
Crossing over.
Taking an unfamiliar territory.
Walking in my assignment.
Healed... with purpose in mind.
In Jesus' name... Amen.

From Broken to Builder

We, as a people, have become used to working from a broken place—building from brokenness rather than victory. What is victory? Victory is the defeat of an enemy; it also means success. James 1:4 tells us, "But let patience have her perfect work, that ye may be perfect and entire, wanting nothing." This underscores the patience needed to build yourself so that ministry work can be done with excellence.

Second Corinthians 4:7 (NKJV) states, "But we have this treasure in earthen vessels, that the excellence of the power may be of God, and not of us."

We are God's masterpiece, and we carry His treasure. There is a message in every work—His perfect work in us. Ephesians 2:10 declares, *"For we are God's masterpiece, His workmanship, created in Christ Jesus for good works, which God prepared beforehand that we should walk in them."* Psalm 139:13-14 reminds us, "For You created my inmost being; You knit me together in my mother's womb. Praise You because I am fearfully and wonderfully made; Your works are wonderful; I know that full well."

You will no longer let your wounds shape your purpose. Yes, our troubles, pain, and the different experiences we've gone through are the backdrop of what God uses for His glory—to help others and guide them into their destiny. But we are not walking in wounded victory. We are walking triumphantly in victory, not still bleeding, and pretending. We are healed, whole, and now we can build—and that building is sufficient for others to come in, experience God in a new way, and it contains and supports what God has used you to build.

Think of the story of Noah. Out of the clear blue, he received a vision to preserve God's people, regardless of whether anyone took heed to it or not, which they did not. Only his family was saved. Our responsibility is to hear the voice of the Lord, obey the voice of the Lord, and watch other lives change.

So, even if you were broken, it wasn't disastrous. Life didn't end. It is a continuation of what God has done and will continue to do, and you can pass that legacy on to others. Life doesn't stop at broken places; it continues in rebuilding.

Build on. Build strong.

ABOUT THE AUTHOR

Crystal Love, a native of Baltimore, is a resolute mother, Elder, and Prophet within the Christian community. She committed her life to the Lord in 1997 at the age of seventeen and was called to ministry at 20. With 25 years of ministry experience, Crystal currently serves as an Elder at Kingdom Worship Center in Baltimore, MD, under the leadership of Bishop Gregory Dennis and Pastor Tonya Dennis. Enthusiastic about community service, Crystal volunteers in

Homeless shelters, teaches at women's transitional homes, engages in outreach and evangelism, and hosts empowerment events to uplift and encourage people to walk in their God-given callings. In 2011, she founded Holistic Ministries to meet individuals' comprehensive spiritual, emotional, social, and physical needs. Holistic Ministries, Inc. is a para-church affiliate of Kingdom Fellowship Covenant Ministries, Inc., under the leadership of her spiritual father, Archbishop Ralph Dennis. An author of several books promoting healing and wholeness, Crystal holds a bachelor's degree in Pastoral Counseling, which equips her to help others recover through the power of the Holy Spirit. Her ministry reflects her deep commitment to assisting individuals to discover their purpose in Jesus Christ and to further the expansion of the Kingdom of God.

"When Jesus saw him lie, and knew that he had been now a long time in that case, he saith unto him, wilt thou be made whole?"- John 5:6

Crystal Love's
Book Collection

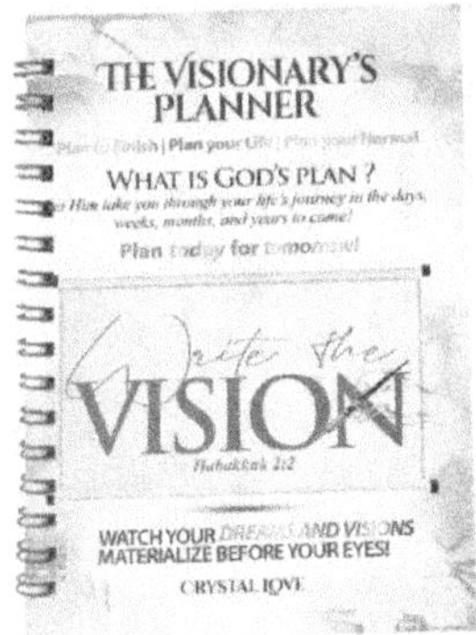

POSITIONING
EQUIPPING
MANTLING
"THE REVEAL"
Crystal Love
kindle

BROKEN TO
BUILD
BY CRYSTAL LOVE

CRYSTAL LOVE
BROKEN TO
BUILD

CRYSTAL LOVE
BROKEN TO
BUILD
BIBLE STUDY CURRICULUM

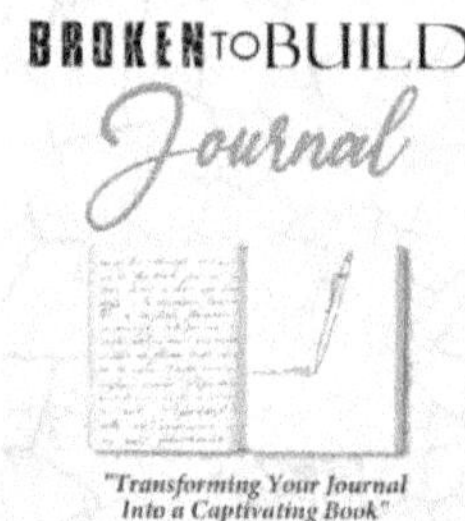
BROKEN TO BUILD
Journal
"Transforming Your Journal
Into a Captivating Book"
CRYSTAL LOVE

<u>For more books and updates</u>

🌐 crystallove-theauthor.com

🌐 holisticministrielove.com

✉ clove@holisticministrieslove.com

f facebook.com/CrystalCeriseLove

📷 instagram.com/holisticministrieslove